Call of the

KEW APPLE

and other stories

CONRAD ROMULD

GRANVILLE ISLAND
PUBLISHING

Text and cover design by Ruby Pearl Productions.
Illustrations and cover artwork by Paul Dwillies.

Library and Archives Canada Cataloguing in Publication

Romuld, Conrad
        Call of the Kew Apple, and other stories / Conrad Romuld.

ISBN 978-1-894694-83-4

        I. Title.

PS8635.O48C34 2010   C813'.6   C2010-905067-3

Granville Island Publishing
212 -1656 Duranleau
Granville Island
Vancouver, BC
Canada V6H 3S4
www.granvilleislandpublishing.com

Come be my love and live with me,
On my quarter-section,
I have a soddy, ten by twelve,
Awaiting your inspection.

Contents

Acknowledgements

My wife, Rita, well deserves my sincere thanks for her part in the creation of this book. Her contribution to whatever entertainment is found in these pages is as real as my own and I want to acknowledge her unstinting support.

As well, I must pay tribute to the team of congenial professionals at Granville Island Publishing who know exactly what to do with a manuscript once it has turned up on their doorstep. Under their tactful direction and with their actual contributions in editing, illustrating, designing and marketing, I travelled unscathed through a world completely new to me. That team includes editor Gordon Thomas, illustrator Paul Dwillies, designer Vici Johnstone and publicist David Litvak. To all of them, my sincere thanks.

Hey! Read this First

When I first began to think about writing *Call of the Kew Apple*, I intended to write something completely original and, indeed, that is how I started out. But there I was, huffing and puffing my way into my ninth decade, boxed in by a lifetime's accumulation of books, with bits and pieces of each swirling around in my head, clamoring to get out to look for a new home on a fresh white page. What was I to do?

I couldn't help it. Some fragments escaped to settle somewhere in this book. As you read, you will come across a familiar thought, a phrase or a line fitted as seamlessly as I could manage into a stylish new context. Whenever this happens, I hope you can react, not with vexation, but with a cry of glad recognition and you might be prompted to look up a literary acquaintance from your youth. You might find that some of that boring hodgepodge you groaned over in high school has miraculously become something good to read.

An acquaintance from my distant past is Paul Hiebert's *Sarah Binks.* What I have tried to do with my book, Paul Hiebert did with his sixty years ago. And he did it better. I respectfully tip my hat to a great writer and, as it has oft been said, "Imitation is the sincerest form of flattery." So now, read on.

Call of the Kew Apple

The Life, Times and Poetry of Lancelot McDough

For far too long, the poetic genius of Lancelot McDough has gone unheralded and unsung. Modest to a degree rarely seen among poets, McDough was content to have his immortal lines read only from hand-written manuscripts sparsely distributed among friends or heard no further afield than in the local schools or in one or another of the community halls located in and around Banshee, Saskatchewan, the hometown that was both his inspiration and his nemesis.

His was the golden age of poetry in Canada, with poets basking in the kind of public adulation currently enjoyed

only by hard rock superstars. They were so sought after by important hostesses that even a minor poet hardly ever had to dine with anyone who didn't own at least one top hat. Leading poets could easily afford to hire a private train to criss-cross the country from town to town, declaiming their odes and sonnets as they went. From Halifax to Victoria, concert halls and churches bulged with excited fans who had gathered to see Bliss Carmen clad in cape and beret, Pauline Johnson arrayed in her feathered war bonnet and Frederick George Scott swathed in Union Jacks.

These public readings had such effect on the populace that little boys took to filching their mothers' best table-cloths because, just as little boys now need a cape to play "Batman," little boys then needed a cape to play "poet." Several generations of turkeys went to the chopping block bereft of their tail feathers because several generations of little farm girls had already fashioned them into fanciful representations of Pauline Johnson's majestic headdress. And young men gallantly responded to Frederick George Scott's stentorian calls to duty by blithely dashing off to war in Africa or Asia or wherever else an ever-expanding Empire might need them. "We must go," they proclaimed. "We've already won Hong Kong, and the rest of China will soon be ours. The Empire forever! God save the King!"

Though our only reward be the thrust of a sword
And a bullet in heart or brain,
What matters one gone, if the flag float on,
And Britain be Lord of the Main.

From "The Colours of the Flag"
—F.G. Scott

Foremost among poets of that era was Sarah Binks, the Sweet Songstress of Saskatchewan. Binks's career is without parallel in Canada's literary history. In her lilting iambs and dauntless dactyls she stands alone, faithfully replicating the timeless rhythms of life on the farm: the comforting *SHOOSH-shoosh SHOOSH-shoosh SHOOSH-shoosh* that signals peace and plenty in the milking shed, the put-put-put-WHACK, put-put-put-WHACK of the Model T Ford jacked up to power the wood-splitter, or the soothing rattle of the north kitchen window as it responds to the caresses of the December wind. A master of metonymy and synecdoche, she is admired equally for her deft use of prosopopeia and polyptoton as well as, especially in her later years, for her bold defiance of rhyme and reason. For her, fame came early and the Sweet Songstress persona came to fill the prairie sky from horizon to horizon, like a great golden cloud that drizzled insight and inspiration onto the parched souls below.

Ironically, although he lived through this period and wrote almost constantly, McDough never shared in the bountiful lifestyle enjoyed by his contemporaries. He simply did not publish. It has been suggested that he was so over-awed by the towering presence of Sarah Binks that he felt his own lines to be unworthy of notice in a world dominated by so great a figure. This sense of unworthiness might have had its origin when his first tentative submission was summarily rejected by the poetry editor of *Mare et Père, the Bilingual Horsebreeders' Gazette.*

But genius will not be denied. Hand-written or crudely duplicated copies of McDough's work still survive to be passed from person to person or to be posted on walls or windows. Favourite pieces are being recited whenever a few devotees can find each other in that vast emptiness that is Saskatchewan. Day by day, this poetic ferment has grown and more and more of the poems, once thought lost, are coming to light. It is tragic beyond belief that this great voice should have been muzzled when it had so many turgid lines pent up within like the foaming energy in a jug of rhubarb wine. It is this author's fervent hope that this book will trigger the catharsis that will see McDough's words, like a thousand whirlwinds, sweep across Canada into every household to become as familiar as "He shoots! He scores!"

One can't help but speculate on what the result might have been if only bumbling circumstance had not kept Saskatchewan's two literary lions apart. They were close contemporaries. They were not greatly separated by geography. The distance from Banshee to the Binks farm near Quagmire could be covered in about two hours by motorcar or, at most, a day by horse and buggy. If benign fortune could have mated these two blazing talents, the resulting conflagration would have engulfed the world, reducing to ashes a thousand years of accumulated poesy.

It is not known just where or when Lancelot McDough made his first appearance on this earth. His parents, Skeeter and Flossie McDough, born tricksters and career drifters, with a toddler son in tow, and probably barely one step ahead of The Law, turned up in the pioneer village of Banshee, shabby additions to the influx of settlers pouring in to the new province of Saskatchewan.

Early in her motherhood, perhaps sensing that her husband would never do anything to give their son a hand up in life, Flossie felt the need to do what she could to make up for the perceived deficiency. Accordingly, as soon as the new

Church of the Glorious Resurrection opened its doors to the faithful, she was there to have her son baptized with his very own name. Until then, the boy had answered to a variety of epithets, none of them calculated to enhance his place in society. Hoping to make up for past neglect, Flossie saddled her son with the most distinguished names that she could think of. That Sunday, he became Lancelot (for nobility of soul) Rockefeller (for wealth and social position) McDough (for all that he would ever get from his father). Her duty done, Flossie resigned herself to a slatternly existence as the junior partner in her husband's futile easy-money schemes.

With each new scheme turning out to be even more futile than the last and with the wolves circling ever nearer, the McDoughs were forced to accept employment as caretakers of the very church in which their son had just been baptized. All might have gone well had Skeeter not tried to use the church boiler room as a distillery. As inept at moonshining as he was at honest labour, Skeeter succeeded only in blowing up his apparatus.

The explosion was barely powerful enough for the church to experience a giant hiccup that left it sitting slightly askew on its foundation. However, in the confines of the boiler room, the effects were devastating, but cleansing. Both Flossie and Skeeter were rendered as dead as Christmas turkeys, thereby sparing the village what would have been a pair of enduring social problems. But that left little Lancelot Rockefeller McDough somehow to be disposed of.

With his parents having been dispatched to a better world, poor little Lancelot was left alone in this one. Homeless and forlorn, he was much in need of love and pity, but was getting precious little of either, especially not from the aggrieved brethren of the Church of the Glorious Resurrection. What was to be done?

The first to step forward, albeit reluctantly, was Tyrone Callaghan, the bachelor proprietor of Banshee's only year-round recreational facility, Callaghan's Billiards and Tobacco Products Ltd., otherwise known simply as "the poolroom." Callaghan felt obliged to help out in this sorry circumstance because he secretly acknowledged some responsibility for the McDoughs ever having come to Banshee.

Flossie, the offspring of a distant relative living in Nebraska, had written to Callaghan ostensibly to inquire about opportunities in Saskatchewan. To his later regret, Callaghan replied with a letter urging her to come to Saskatchewan to check out the opportunities for herself

and, even more regrettably, had enclosed money for railroad fare. Little Lancelot, the grubby detritus left over from this exchange of correspondence, was now someone's unwelcome responsibility. Callaghan offered to take the boy in. No one else spoke up, except to offer congratulations.

Callaghan never regretted his charitable impulse. Lancelot took readily to life on Banshee's Main Street, for that is where the poolroom was located. It was in the middle of the block with the Methodist church on one side and the Almighty Bank of Canada on the other. Directly across the street was Harry Wong's Happy Dragon Café, which, Lancelot soon learned, was a good place to hang out. Strung along the rest of Main Street's two blocks were the livery barn at one end, the CPR station at the other, and in between the Celestial Palace Hotel, Casey's General Store (which had in stock everything from a tin of baking powder to a wedding gown or a set of buggy harness), Hockenpacker's Bakery, Hansen's Beauty Salon and Shoe Repair, and the Banshee Town Office, which served as well as the headquarters for the Rural Municipality of Brouhaha. Around the corner to the north was the Post Office and, to the south, the central office and switchboard for the Banshee Rural Telephone Company.

Not to be overlooked, beside the Happy Dragon Café was a tidy one-storey building with barred windows. It was the Government Liquor Store, where for forty cents, one could buy a bottle of Ontario-made sherry or port. Or, if half a dozen good friends could raise an additional dollar-sixty, they could buy an entire gallon of the concoction, take it across the railway tracks down by the stockyard and, sitting in the shade, get gloriously tight.

Lancelot was assigned space and a cot in a corner of Callaghan's living quarters above the poolroom. There he usually slept and sometimes ate when there wasn't something better on the immediate horizon. Townsfolk cheerfully accepted raising him as a community responsibility. Everyone looked after him, picking him up, dusting him off, wiping his nose, encouraging, consoling, scolding, and when provocation was sufficiently dire, spanking him.

A key figure in this shared responsibility was Harry Wong of the Happy Dragon Café. Harry had acquired his culinary skills as a cook's helper on a railroad construction crew as the track snaked its way through the mountains. Then one day he appeared in Banshee introducing himself as the new owner of the Happy Dragon. The previous owner silently disappeared. Early conjecture was, and the belief quickly grew, that Harry had won the business in Calgary by playing some mysterious Oriental version of poker.

Harry and Banshee loved each other. He was genial and generous and patrons thronged his premises every day. Lancelot became a fixture among them and benefited hugely from being under Harry's watchful eye. He was brought up by Harry probably more than he was by Callaghan.

Lancelot roamed the village, making friends everywhere he went, foraging for food, which was plentiful and freely shared. Bright, observant and a careful listener, he became the repository for village gossip which, on his rounds, he innocently passed on, thereby making himself all the more welcome everywhere he went.

He was almost unaware of the distinguished names he bore because he so seldom heard them. In Banshee, everyone knew him simply as "Lance." When he learned that a lance was a chivalric weapon, he puffed out his chest for a moment and savoured a little of the advantage that his mother had hoped for.

Later on, when he came to understand that a lance was also a phallic symbol with its own chivalric history, he puffed out his chest for a longer moment and gained even more of that same psychological boost. As Flossie had correctly surmised, it helps a boy to have a name he can be proud of.

Lance hadn't needed and almost never heard his surname until he started school. Then, as institutions and bureaucracies thrive on forms to fill out, his surname had to come out from the shadows. It helps too if a boy's surname is one he can be proud of, but Lance was uncertain about his because he was never sure of how to say it and he had no parental authority to advise him.

McDough? Should the *ough* rhyme with *rough* or *cough?* Then what about *bough* or *though?* Or *through?* Lance didn't waste time pondering the imponderable. A name didn't matter. He would use his surname only when he had to. There was ample satisfaction in *Lance.* That was all the name he would use.

Lance had never learned any nursery rhymes from his parents, most probably because they had never heard any themselves. But, from the first time he heard "Jack Be Nimble," he was enchanted. He learned rhymes in the homes of his playmates. He learned from little girls chanting rhymes as they skipped on the front sidewalks. He was so stimulated by seeing a cluster of girls engaged with their skipping ropes he could not forbear, but had to thrust himself into their company. As it turned out, he quickly became just as good at skipping as any girl. He could skip backward just as well as forward, on either leg just as well as on both and, with two girls twirling the rope, could rotate in either direction as he skipped.

As time went on, this easy association with girls progressed to include a wider range of activities, some of them less public than skipping on the front sidewalk. Inclement weather sometimes drove the children indoors where they could engage in that wonderful age-old favourite, "Let's Pretend." In their various roles in these improvised dramas, the children came to know much more about each other than would have been the case had they confined their play to skipping on public sidewalks.

In Banshee, it is widely believed that Lance was composing verse even before he started school. There are several rhymes and skipping chants still heard in the village that are not heard anywhere else and that the few remaining elders attribute to him. Among the earliest are these, the first one chronicling a series of domestic vexations, something Lance might have observed in the home of a friend.

Sarah Burnt the Porridge

Sarah burnt the porridge,
Sally broke a plate,
Susan spilled the buttermilk,
So now they'll all be late.

The next one is about a girl named Melissa whose reputation still lingers.

Melissa

If you ever have a chance,
You should see Melissa dance,
Jumping over rhubarb plants,
While not wearing underpants.

When little boys are not being curious about what's under girls' skirts, they enjoy seeing dignity upended.

A Big Bellyflopper

A blooper a blopper,
A big bellyflopper,
The preacher fell down in a puddle,
By jingle by jangle,
Oh boy, what a tangle!
Now everything's all in a muddle.

The pioneer housewife had to contend with many crises.

Maggots in the Oatmeal

Maggots in the oatmeal,
Weevils in the rice,
Mice drowned in the buttermilk,
Now ain't that mighty nice!

Geese can have the oatmeal,
Ducks can have the rice,
Pigs can have the buttermilk,
But who will have my lice?

Both the poolroom and the Happy Dragon Café had candy counters to which Lance had easy access. The wealth thus attained, he shared judiciously with other boys, but when it came to girls, he learned early to bargain for favours.

Candy Is Dandy

Jellybeans, peppermints, green and white,
Grape flavour bubblegum lasts overnight,
Gum drops, humbugs an' black licorice
What do you want for just one kiss?

Our research has not yet revealed what an older Lance might have negotiated in exchange for a whole bag of caramels.

One rhyme in particular, from McDough's pre-school period, deserves a much closer look. Only four lines long, it gives eloquent expression to one of the most perplexing and enduring problems affecting life on Planet Earth.

Hippety Tippety Poppety Poo

Hippety tippety poppety poo,
Skunk's in the henhouse. What can I do?
Have him for lunch with choc'lit fondue.
Hippety tippety poppety poo.

The first line sets a wide stage. Those ten lilting syllables break free from the confines of human speech. They don't immediately appear to say anything in particular. Yet they say everything because they represent the universality of language, the language of all creatures great and small, from whales to warble flies, the language of all earthlings. The second line puts Earth under a microscope and zooms in on a crisis and a desperate cry for help. There's a skunk in the hen-house. "What *can I* do?" Not "What *should I* do?" for there is no established protocol for dealing with an emergency of this nature. The tension is so great one can almost smell it. Then comes an answer, and such a humane and welcome solution it is. Of course! Have him for lunch!

But relaxation is brief. In only a moment the reader detects the artful ambiguity of *"Have* him for lunch." Is the skunk to be invited or eaten? What appeared to be an easy way out is only a blind alley. The fourth line's return to "Hippety tippety poppety poo" is a return to the language of all creation and indicates the universality and timelessness of life's great dilemmas. Why can't we warm up to skunks? Skunks, when left to themselves, are gregarious and playful. They are loyal to their spouses, conscientious and loving parents and are becomingly modest about their sartorial elegance. Really, they are among the most engaging of God's creatures. Yet they are vilified and shunned by all the others. Why this antipathy?

Lance McDough was indeed a genius. In these four lines, this five-year-old prodigy delivers truth, more profound and more pervasive than Shakespeare achieved with all his great tragedies. Plainly stated, it is that antipathy toward skunks is like sin. It is real and it is permanent. It is quickly learned and never forgotten. A truth so fundamental can't be stated more succinctly or gracefully than in this immortal poem.

Once Lance started school and grasped the rudiments of phonics, almost at once, he became a voracious reader. A voracious reader, he also became an indefatigable writer, leaving here and there, hundreds of lyrical gems written with pencil on odd scraps of paper. Unfortunately, only a few of them have survived, many having been used to start the morning fire in the kitchen stove or for some other mundane household purpose. However, those that escaped the flames are ample testimony to his future greatness.

Rural children learn early that, on a farm, a pet is not quite what it might be to city folk. Cats are there to catch mice and dogs to herd cattle. A lamb is valued for its chops and a heifer for its butterfat potential. If an animal fails to meet expectations, its life expectancy can be surprisingly short. "My Puppy" reflects a child's laconic acceptance of this practical lesson in agricultural economics.

My Puppy

My puppy killed a chicken,
Which is a mortal sin.
He's frolicking around the yard,
With feathers on his chin.
That poor dumb puppy doesn't know
The trouble that he's in.

In rather the same vein is a child's dispassionate view of the relationship between cat and mouse.

Kittens at Play

Oh wippity woppity wee
'Tis the funniest sight to see.
The mama cat brought her kittens a mouse,
And now they're chasing it all over the house.

The mouse tries to hide under a chair,
But claws and sharp teeth already are there.

He stops to look for the best place to run,
While the kittens are having such jolly good fun.

Miss Puss tosses the mouse aloft to her brother,
He bobbles and slaps it across to another,
Who pins the mouse down with a paw on its tail,
What am I bid? This mouse is for sale!

But these cat-and-mouse games never last long,
The cats always win, for they never guess wrong.
The mouse will soon tire of this crazy bunch,
And the game will be over when it's time for lunch.

In summer there can be many reasons for feeling good.

Summer Days

By golly, by jingo, by gee!
Nobody is better than me.
I hit a home run and came first in the race,
And girls like to chase me all over the place,
I got new running shoes and a two-wheeler bike,
And a dollar to spend on whatever I like.

Further examples of Lance's early work remained extant in written form for several years on the walls of Banshee's Literary Archives Building, which doubled as the comfort facility for the CPR station. Usually limericks or four-line ditties made up of rhyming couplets, these gems beguiled many a drop-in visitor until the building was struck by lightning and burned to the ground.

Throughout his childhood and early adolescence, Lance continued to roam the streets of Banshee, running errands, delivering groceries, helping with minor household chores and generally making himself agreeable to the younger of the village matrons. In two or three instances, he made himself so agreeable that sometimes supper was late.

The most whispered about of these few instances starred Mrs. Edwina Topdrawer-Wideacre, his patron and mentor, the third but certainly not the least of the influences that shaped Lance's life. She was English, the daughter of a minor civil servant, had been reared in genteel poverty, became a nurse and then married a wounded officer from a Canadian regiment.

Her husband, Reginald Topdrawer-Wideacre, had been born and raised in England, but sometime late in the reign of Edward VII, at the urgent and uncompromising insistence of his parents, emigrated to Canada. Rumour of the day was that his emigration was necessary to escape a duel with a member of the Royal family. By some strange quirk of fate, he settled in Banshee where, thanks to a regular remittance from home, he was able to stay idle and intoxicated until the beginning of World War I.

During a short period of relative sobriety, he wandered into a recruiting depot in Regina where, on the strength of his brief attendance at a prestigious public school and his ability to converse knowledgeably about horses, he was offered a commission in a cavalry regiment. In the army, his personal peculiarities weren't of enough consequence to impede his progress from one rank to the next. By the time he got to the battlefields in France, he was a major. That was when an exploding artillery shell blew him out of his saddle and out of the battlefields forever. Hospitalized in England, his frail psyche damaged beyond repair, he was nursed by Edwina Cumpstone, who, against everyone's advice, married him.

War hero or not, invalid or not, married or not, Reginald Topdrawer-Wideacre was still not welcome in the bosom of his family, not on their vast estate nor, indeed, anywhere in England. With a modest increase in his remittance and now with a disability pension and a wife, he returned to Banshee.

To her marriage, Edwina brought an unconquerable spirit and an irrepressible sense of humour, both of which served her well in her new life in rural Saskatchewan. In material goods, her dowry was limited to a few out-of-fashion dresses, some bits of inexpensive jewelry and a set of leather-bound volumes which, she liked to point out, offered a generous sampling of the best in English poetry from Chaucer to Tennyson. Edwina cherished the books, but Lance read them from cover to cover, over and over again.

Edwina was kind-hearted and generous with her time and attention, but she had to make life bearable for herself. Reginald, hapless and hopeless, was just a thing that had to be fed and watered. She had to keep him alive and functioning to some degree because his monthly cheques were their only income. She resolved that she would look after herself at least as well as she looked after her husband. And she would simply stare down anyone who seemed to look askance at her initiatives.

Reginald was encouraged to follow his natural inclinations and to lie late abed, preferably until noon. Edwina used the morning to do her housework and her shopping. At noon, she and Reginald would share a simple meal, lunch for her, but breakfast for him. After the meal, Edwina would run a critical eye over her husband and tick off her mental checklist: shoes shined? socks matched? fly buttoned? shirt tail in? tie unspotted? Next, she would count out a dollar in dimes with the injunction that he make them last until teatime. That done, she would take him out the front door and point him in the direction of the Celestial Palace Hotel, where beer was ten cents a glass.

Two or three times a week, about this time of day, Lance would turn up. He might begin the afternoon with something seasonal — weeding, raking or shovelling — but would soon be admitted indoors where he sat at the kitchen table and either read or wrote. Edwina recognized Lance's emerging talents and nurtured them every way she could. Not only did she give him a place to write, she provided him with the necessities: regular purchases of pencils; and the Powwow School Exercise Book — thick scribblers of lined newsprint with a picture of an Indian encampment on the front cover and an intimidating array of mathematical tables on the back. Lance was such a prolific writer that Edwina had to buy a dozen or so scribblers almost every month. As each one was filled, it was numbered and dated and put away for safe-keeping.

Time would pass all too quickly on these afternoons and, as six o'clock approached, Edwina would know that her husband's supply of dimes would be exhausted and his perceptions would be too blurred for him to find his way home without assistance. Lance would put his writing materials aside and proceed to the hotel bar where he would rouse Reginald from his lethargy and lead him home for Edwina's evening ministrations. Through this domestic *entente cordiale,* Lance gained an early insight into tender human relationships — always an inspiration to poets.

On his way home to the poolroom, Lance would always take with him the current Powwow Exercise Book so that he could continue writing far into the night. But when each one was filled, he would never fail to deliver it to Edwina in order that she could see to its preservation. As the books began to accumulate, there was no longer enough space on shelves or in drawers. Edwina dealt with that problem by using corrugated cardboard cartons obtained from Casey's store. Cartons that had held twenty-four tins of Fertile Valley Tomato Juice would hold exactly fifty books. By the time of Lance's untimely death, Edwina had cartons stacked ceiling high lining two walls of her back bedroom.

There they remained for almost forty years until Edwina's death in 1985. Then, the contents of her house became the object of a long-drawn-out civil suit between the Topdrawer-Wideacre family in England and a coterie of Saskatchewan literati. The Topdrawer-Wideacres thought the books might be Edwina's or even Reginald's personal diary and feared a revival of the scandal that had so titillated Edwardian England. The Saskatchewan side, led by Dr. Alma Ergot, Dean of Arts at Buffalo Jump University, had got wind of the actual content of the boxes and hoped to win acclaim as the experts who discovered Lancelot McDough. They fought to prevent the removal of the boxes from Saskatchewan on the grounds that they and their contents were a national treasure.

That tangle of lawsuits is soon to be resolved. A compromise has been worked out whereby the Topdrawer-Wideacres will be protected from a century-old scandal and Saskatchewan academics will have sole access to these precious manuscripts.

Until that happens and our scholars have perused and processed this treasure trove, the world will have to be satisfied with those scattered fragments of McDough's work that somehow escaped loss or destruction during eight decades of Saskatchewan's turbulent history.

Among those loose pages that researchers have managed to gather together are many that reveal Lance's fixation on an imaginary Eden. Over half bear touching lyrics about a world known only to him — the Kew Apple Valley — a mystic Avalon, a pastoral paradise inhabited by beautiful people.

Why Kew Apple? Where did the name come from? Lance certainly did not find it on a map of Saskatchewan. Dr. Wilda Hemp, Professor of Linguistics and Water Divining at Thunderhead Agricultural College, having researched this question for decades, has developed a persuasive explanation based on an incident that happened when Lance was eleven years old.

When Lance was in Grade Five, his teacher was a young man named Engledink Humperbump, the son of immigrant parents who were part of a German-speaking community near the Alberta border. Mr. Humperbump was justifiably proud of his proficiency in English, which he had managed to acquire in almost complete isolation from anyone who actually spoke the language. He had a fine voice, deep and resonant, and was especially fond of reciting poetry or reading it aloud which he could do in English almost as well as he did in German.

One day, Mr. Humperbump was deeply engrossed in reading to his class a poem by Pauline Johnson, Canada's renowned Indian poetess. Somewhere in the depths of the piece he was reading, Mr. Humperbump was confronted by something that was neither English nor German. *Qu'Appelle.* Enraptured by the drama of the moment and by the sound of of his own voice, Mr. Humperbump didn't even pause to consider. He did the best he could with what he saw. He saw *Qu'Appelle,* but he said *Kew Apple.* A few lines further on, there it was again. Twice. *Kew Apple! Kew Apple!* Mr. Humperbump's ringing declamation reverberated throughout the school, and his contribution to Saskatchewan English became indelibly imprinted onto Lance's impressionable young mind.

There it was. For Lance, Kew Apple was a place with an existence as real and undeniable as his own. It was a place that he would write about.

Call of the Kew Apple

In the broad Kew Apple Valley
Is where I long to be,
Lounging in a hammock,
'Neath a tall kew apple tree.

It boasts a mighty river,
Flowing fast and free,
And stately ships ply to and fro,
From mountains to the sea.

Tower'd castles line both shores,
Built there by Sioux and Cree,
With profits from the fur trade,
Where they live like royalty.

Dark-eyed maidens clad in buckskin,
And beaded finery,
Flit gracefully from tree to tree,
And smile invitingly.

I would rise and gird myself,
And fly there like a whiz,
Straight to that valley paradise,
But I don't know where it is.

But I don't know where it is! With this line, the reader can only marvel at the breadth and profundity of this young poet's cosmic consciousness and his empathy with those legions of poets who preceded him in their endless quest for *The Altogether.* What does it profit a man to know the *What* but not the *Where?* The *Who* but not the *When?* or the *How* but not the *Why?*

The next poem catches Lance in an ebullient mood. The page on which it was written is a bit sticky and is discoloured with what appears to be a trace of treacle pudding; a favourite of Lance's, which Edwina sometimes made for special afternoons.

Go Down to Kew in Apple Time

Go down to Kew in apple time, in apple time, in apple time,
Go down to Kew in apple time. It must be out there somewhere.
The valley has a lovely view of apple trees, but few of yew,
And few of you have been to Kew when blossom time is due there.
The blossoms are a true blue hue even when the dew is new,
And morning tea has yet to brew. Will orange pekoe do for you?

Apples here are all too few, often old and never new. I never knew
That apples grew down there in Kew. Kew apples are a joy to chew,
And are so jolly good for you, if you boil or bake or barbeque.
Go down to Kew in apple time in apple time in apple time,
Go down to Kew in apple time. I hope that you can find it.

"Such imagery! Such breathtaking polyptoton!" exclaimed
Dr. Ergot upon reading this masterpiece in *Ovine and Bovine,
the Herdsman's Quarterly.* "It is so original, yet has the appealing ring of familiarity. I almost feel that I've read it before."

Lance was everyone's friend. He knew everything about
everybody, partly because he had a poet's inquiring mind
and partly because people tended not to notice that he was
within earshot during those moments of fine careless rapture
associated with knocking back a magnum of chokecherry
wine. With remarkable frequency, Lance seemed to find
himself in situations where lips had been loosened or inhi-
bitions lowered. The information he gleaned would find its
way into verse.

After a good June rain, optimism among farmers is as
contagious as hog cholera. "The Farmer Is King" must have
been written after a three-day soaker.

The Farmer Is King

Oh ring a ding ding! The farmer is king,
Of his ox and his plow and his field,
He gambols all day midst windrows of hay,
Ecstatic that he's so well-heeled.

He outfoxes bankers and lawyers,
Every day of the year,
And strews their bones in his pasture,
And toasts them with Chateau d'Yquier.

His granaries are bursting with riches,
A huge crop is coming again,
He'll buy another Mercedes,
And wash his feet in champagne.

Every community had a generous sprinkling of bachelor farmers, men of every age, size and disposition who had acquired a homestead, but for one reason or another, had not succeeded in acquiring a wife. These men often resorted to the printed word to make their first approach. Sometimes they advertised and sometimes they tried the "Lonely Hearts" page of a farm newspaper. A brief exchange of letters might lead to something like this:

Come Be My Love

Come be my love and live with me,
On my quarter-section,
I have a soddy, ten by twelve,
Awaiting your inspection.

Its walls are thick, the floor smooth-packed,
The roof is thatched with grass,
The window frees the wayward breeze,
'Cause I haven't any glass.

We'll spend our days in joyful toil,
Unconcerned with riches,
With naught to do with bankers who,
Are rotten sonsabitches.

In winter come the whispering winds,
And gentle fall of snow,
We'll bring our ox in for the night,
When the mercury sinks too low.

He'll lie close by our straw-filled bed,
Where mice play hide and seek,
His body heat will warm our feet,
While we snuggle cheek to cheek.

When morning comes, we three will rise,
To share a gruel confection,

And you will see that life with me,
Is absolute perfection.

So be my love and live with me.
You are my burning passion,
This wealth of mine will all be thine,
In true conjugal fashion.

In the next poem, the long-distance courtship has apparently proceeded to the point where the prospective bride has come to the farm to inspect the facilities it has to offer. The simple, yet delightful, "Sanctum Sanctorum" gives full expression to the mystique of the two-holer.

Sanctum Sanctorum

Come down past the garden, Maud,
Beyond yon clump of birch,
Where stands a humble edifice,
More sacred than a church.

I make a solemn pilgrimage,
Once or twice a day,
To contemplate the Universe,
And problems to allay.

'Tis only on the morrow,
That we two shall wed,
And you should view this sanctum,
Ere evening prayers are said.

You'll note the architect,
Saw two sate side by side,
A place for me and one for thee,
When you're my blushing bride

The ambience is perfect
For thoughtful conversation,
Of shoes and ships and sealing wax
And our sublime vocation.

Here we would consider,
The economic factors,
The price of oats and winter coats,
And Massey Harris tractors.

So there we'd sit and I admit,
'Tis cold here in December
Each moment passed 'midst winter's blast
Is something you'll remember.

Still from Lance's juvenile period, "The King" hints at his incipient republicanism. The king under scrutiny would be George V who reigned during World War I. During his reign, love of God, the Monarchy and the Empire was still the prime motivating force in the hearts and minds of loyal Canadians. Friends feared that Lance's increasingly subversive comments, especially those reflecting his growing sympathy for Irish nationalism, might lead to trouble, but no one expected that, when it came, the reaction would be so sudden and so final.

The King

God save our good gracious king,
'Tis said he's wondrous wise,
'Way smarter than the Pope,
And all those other guys.

He wears a fancy uniform
With gold medals 'cross his chest,
Whate'er he did to win them,
No one has ever guessed.

He has a million dollars,
Kept under lock and key,
He spends them on his girlfriends,
But not on you and me.

He looks a little wobbly,
For he is growing old,
His crown sits heavy on his head,
'Cause it's made of solid gold.

The Prince of Wales is waiting,
To occupy the throne,
The King should watch behind him,
And not go out alone.

Life on the frontier was always dangerous and was sometimes cut short by the totally unexpected. Untimely death might be shrugged off with a joke or a laconic comment.

Requiem for Grampa Sigurdson

Grampa died a tragic death,
It really was too bad,
It happened in the dark of night,
And made us feel so sad.

No one was to blame,
No one was at fault,
His death occurred because,
Porcupines love salt.

Salt for them is hard to find,
For they don't have salt shakers,
But where there is the slightest bit,
They are greedy takers.

Wooden-handled tools,
Held with a sweaty hand,
Axes, hoes and pitchforks,
Are in high demand.

So are wooden toilet seats,
In outdoor privies old,
Infused with salt from sweaty bums,
As much as they can hold.

Every night at bedtime,
It was Grampa's style,
To stroll down to the outhouse,
To meditate awhile.

That night a massive porcupine,
To claim a major find,
Lay stretched across the salty seat,
With nothing on his mind

But to gnaw his fill,
Of this tasty nighttime snack,
When Gramp's bare bottom squashed him down,
The porcupine fought back.

He bit and slashed and flailed his tail,
'Mongst Grampa's private places,
Then out the door forevermore,
To find wide-open spaces.

They lived a dozen miles from town,
Had neither car nor truck,
There was no phone to call for help,
It was such rotten luck.

Grandma got the pliers,
And a quart of rum,
Poured some for him and some for her,
Now Einar, here I come!

Quill removal took till morn,
With Grampa loudly swearing,
With every yank, his spirits sank,
Till he was long past caring.

Grampa lingered near a week,
Just stricken to the heart,
T'wouldn't be so bad, he said,
But it hurts me when I fart.

I have these two requests, my dear,
And, Helga, please don't frown.
Bake lefse for my funeral,
And bury me face down.

With all the available poems written on individual pieces of paper, arranging them into some semblance of chronological order is extremely difficult. Some of the work already presented is clearly infantile and some is better described as juvenile. The poems henceforth will reflect a broader range of experience and a more mature understanding of what this world is all about.

The next poem, "Requiescat," a reflection on Creation, Life, Death and the Everlasting, was inspired by the poet's coming across the mangled corpse of Attila, a locally notorious tomcat.

Requiescat

Requiescat, thou noble cat,
Thy nine lives all are spent.
I watched thee roam the country round,
When thou wert on pleasure bent.
Thy golden orbs did'st pierce the night,
Like Chevy headlights turned on bright.
What demonic hand or eye,
Could shape thy fierce effrontery,
To make a world where old tomcats,
Would'st be the sole aristocrats?

Those who have been privileged to read from that small portion of Lance's work available to the public express amazement at the ease with which he moves from the vernacular of the Banshee poolroom to the elevated diction of seventeenth- or eighteenth-century English poets, sometimes within the same poem. "A marvellous gift," writes Dr. Ergot. "He does it so smoothly that one might almost believe that he doesn't see any difference."

In situations of profound emotion or physical distress, however, he clearly feels the inadequacy of modern parlance and expresses his pain as eloquently as would Donne or Blake or even Shakespeare. The following lament is ample illustration.

Lament on a Urinary Disorder

Oh woe is me! I cannot pee,
I wot not what's amiss,
A valve is locked; my plumbing blocked,
I need, but cannot piss.

Perchance some errant worm or fluke,
A damnèd dam hath built,
Or else my daily forage of flax and lentil porridge,
Hath plugged my drain with silt.

What art? What spell? What purgative or prayer,
Can cure my desp'rate plight? What exercise or pill?
Might I, forsooth, shake something loose,
If I roll down yonder hill?

This cursèd curse is getting worse,
I know not what to think,
Should I ride a bucking bronc,
Or quaff a lethal drink?

Oh blessèd chance! I've wet my pants!
So something worked and I'm uncorked,
And the curst impediment is naught. It's not a dream,
For a noble stream doth tinkle cheerily in the pot.

When Lance was thirteen years old, he was expelled from Sunday School. This happened, not because he had misbehaved, but because he would not accept what he was being taught. He embarrassed his teachers by being openly skeptical. *A burning bush that talks? Maybe there was a radio. Parting the sea? Why didn't they just walk on water? If God cares so much about the little sparrow, why does He let it fall? God knows what I'm thinking? Then why doesn't He strike me dead? God's not doing a very good job. That's what I'm thinking.*

Of course he was sent home for the day, but on the following Sunday, he refused to go back. His absence was quietly accepted by the minister, Rev. Hosea Piltdown, who would rather see a vagrant soul consigned to eternal damnation than have it hanging around his church sowing doubt and discord among his docile followers.

God?

I don't believe in God.
Don't think I ever did.
All I did was just pretend,
And do as I was bid.

So I sang that Jesus loves me,
And prayed my soul should not be lost,
But all the while I did those things,
I kept my fingers crossed.

Thank Who?

Thank God they're safe! They all exclaimed,
It was a dreadful fright.
The house burned down right to the ground,
In the middle of the night.

And the children all are safe!
Thank watchful God for that.
No one even scorched, they say,
But the hired man and the cat.

He woke up in the bunkhouse,
To smell the acrid smoke,
And quick as thought ran to the house,
To rouse the slumb'ring folk.

'Twas God's blessing that he wakened,
We thank the Lord for that.
But whose shirt tail caught on fire,
When he tried to save the cat?

God is good and God is great,
They chant with glowing heart.
But, if that is so, I wonder,
Why He let that fire start.

It is known that Lance wrote many more poems on religious
themes, both before and after his separation from the church.
There should be far more than these two in circulation, but
despite our researchers' best efforts, no more have come to

light. It would seem as if Reverand Piltdown and his thought police have succeeded in a kind of seek and destroy mission. However, the nation can take comfort in the expectation that the Powwow School Exercise Books will yield more than enough to make up for the current lack.

Today's hockey players and their fans, reared in air-conditioned arenas with artificial ice, don't know anything about their game as it was first played in rural Saskatchewan. This tribute is long overdue.

To The Horse

A plea for an Equine Trophy in the NHL

Hail to thee, thou noble steed,
Exemplar of the Clydesdale breed,
Yes, Percherons and Belgians too,
And bucking Broncs of every hue.

You deserve undying fame,
For selfless giving to The Game,
That first was played on frozen ponds,
With wooden sticks, those magic wands

That with a pair of battered skates,
Turned bashful farm boys into hockey greats.
Buzz Boll, Doug Bentley and his brother Max,
And those who followed in their tracks,

Bert Olmstead, Elmer Lach, the Allens, George and Squee,
And the brothers Metz made history,

With skill and will and endless drill. And now,
Take note that Gordie showed us Howe,

To stickhandle, pass and score,
Starting off with nothing more,
Than ambition and a touch of luck,
With home-made stick and horse-made puck.

Without that puck our stars would be,
Just ord'ny guys like you and me,
In this Great Game, the praises sung
Ain't worth as much as frozen dung.

So round, so firm, so tightly packed,
To stay in shape when soundly whacked,
With blistering slapshot, bounce off a stone,
Yet hang together, tough as bone.

From schoolgirl's pony to plowman's horse,
You've earned our gratitude, of course,
For such devotion to The Game,
You should be in the Hall of Fame.

The absolute timelessness of male-female attraction is exemplified in "My Heart Leaps Up." Our male protagonist is speaking for all generations everywhere.

My Heart Leaps Up

My heart leaps up when I espy,
A nubile maiden passing by,

So was it when I was a lad,
And so is it now I'm in my votage,
And pray it last right through my dotage,
Those rosy lips and swaying hips,
Set my heart aglow. With every wiggle,
My hormones jiggle and make me think Romance!
Here comes one now.
Would you care to dance?
Tra la la la la, tra la tra la ...

In Saskatchewan, the spirit of co-operation is as real and everlasting as hailstorms and early frost, and no one is more representative of that spirit than the family of Olaf Strand.

Co-operatively Yours

Olaf Strand was co-operative,
In action, word and thought,
In everything he ever made,
And whatever else he bought.

He joined a farm co-operative,
To buy fuel oil and twine,
And another in the city,
For emeralds and wine.

His grain went to the Pool,
As did his hogs and steers,
To be marketed collectively,
And allay financial fears.

His loyal sons and daughters,
Were faithful to the Code,
They lived and breathed the Co-op Creed,
From which all blessings flowed.

They shared in doing chores,
Like feeding pigs their slop,
And gathering eggs each evening,
From their very own chicken co-op.

Lance's epic, "The Royal Wedding," will rank with the great narratives of world literature. In a biting social satire, the narrator relates a story of class distinction, illicit romance, danger, duplicity, intrigue, enlightenment and final redemption, all unfolding in a rural Saskatchewan setting in little more than twelve hours.

The compelling story is enhanced by the jaunty if somewhat irregular meter and the melodious, if not even more irregular, rhyming couplets. Professor Ergot offers this comment:

The poetic structure reflects the vagaries of farming in Saskatchewan. If you're a farmer, you just get everything settled and running smoothly and then you get a weasel in the henhouse and all hell breaks loose.

The Royal Wedding

When I was a lad, still in my teens,
To keep myself in bacon an' beans,
I took a job at a dollar a day,
On the farm of Senator Clyde MacNeigh.

The farm was one of high repute,
Its steeds were all noble, its lambkins all cute,
Its fields were prolific, its herds were all fat,
And barns were cleaned daily with panache and *éclat*.

A competitive breeder of flora and fauna,
McNeigh'd won many trophies, but not all he's gonna,
For he owns Princess Roona of Rottergodam,
The prettiest heifer e'er seen by man.

Her credentials impeccable, her lineage pure,
She'd conceive only champions, but one first must ensure,
She meets just the right fella with a proud family tree,
Equal at least to her pedigree.

Prince Hendrik van Haarlem lives not far away,
On the splendiferous farm of Schleshwig von Kaye,
With a pedigree longer than verses writ here,
And betrothal contracted since many a year.

So, one sunny morning, it came thus to pass,
That a curious whimsy beset our fair lass,
There was something she wanted, she knew not quite what,
She diddled and daddled, decorum forgot.

Ah, said MacNeigh, I've seen this before,
And our Princess this morning proclaims nothing more,
Than she craves male attention,
To end her abstention,

From procreativity. I'll call up von Kaye,
Who'll brook no delay,
In calling a meeting,
For time is fast fleeting.

Tomorrow Prince Hendrik departs for P.Q.,
But first, we must see that our virginal two
Hold true to our deal for a conjugal tryst,
One that 'tis sworn shall not be missed.

How, you ask, can that be done,
With trucks an' trailers every one
Away in Brandon at the fair,
Leaving us without a wheel to spare.

That matters not a whit,
For the stars say, "This is it."
The planets and her hormones harmonize,
So I'm counting on you guys,

To help the Princess keep this date,
Which happily will consummate,
This lucrative betrothal pact,
So now it's time to act.

A flurry of milkmaids then burst on the scene,
With brushes and bottles and a shampoo machine,
They perfumed and polished, bedecked her with bows,
And beads and brass bangles from T-bone to nose.

When opportunity comes knocking,
There's nothing wrong with walking,
So with just a rope and halter,
We'll lead Princess to the altar.

It's a little far by highway,
But there's an easy byway,
As the crow flies is the route to take,
A cross-country stroll will be a piece of cake.

In view of what he's learned,
And of all the trust he's earned,
This leading role is offered,
To our new Assistant Cowherd.

So get your gear together,
Free Princess from her tether,
And without undue delay,
Get this wedding under way.

Take this pink parasol to shade her from sun,
And put on a clean shirt, if you have one,
Tie rope to the halter and start on your way,
God bless you and keep you this auspicious day.

With glowing heart and solemn will, I led the Bride along,
Past pastures green and waters still, oft breaking into song,
The Princess mooed most plaintively. She sings *Adieu,* I thought,
How wrong I was about those moos I never have forgot.

Her moos were news to attentive ears perked up all o'er the lea,
Of a love-struck bossy feeling saucy and wanting company,
A motley herd clearly heard her message, fair and full,
Among them was a base-born beast, Brutus, a bastard bull.

Ragged, scruffy bovine trash, but agile as a goat,
Horns long and curved like scimitars, a CPR red coat,
He raised his head and cocked his ears, and sniffed the air's portent,
Swished his tail and pawed the earth, assessing that *Come hither* scent.

In his zeal to propagate,
'Twas naught for him to hop a gate,
And I saw him clear it like a deer,
And when he charged at me, my will gave way to fear.

I think that I shall never see,
A sight more welcome than the tree,
Up which I fled. The tree whose leafy arm was spread,
A precious yard o'er el Toro's head.

'Twas an absolute disgrace,
To see Roona rapt in foul embrace,
And Brutus in such fulsome measure,
Wreaking his bestial pleasure,

On sweet Roona of Rottergodam,
My shouts and curses weren't worth a damn,
Brutus simply had his way,
On that bleak and dismal day.

Brutus crowned his quick romance,
With a wild and whirling vict'ry dance,
With hoof and horn tore up the earth,
Hurled sods and clods for all he's worth.

He tore and trampled left and right,
Bucked and bounced with all his might,
And charged the tree that was my perch,
A tall and sturdy clump of birch.

He reared and lunged and rammed his head,
Between twin trunks that had grown to spread,
From a common base to form a V
That trapped him, just as he deserved to be.

His struggles were to no avail,
He could but bawl and flail his tail,
The Princess stood by patiently,
Waiting till I forsook my tree.

The common word was that von Kaye,
Had wedding preparations under way,
With chilled champagne and canapés,
And spitted quail and *crème brûlées.*

I really didn't want to miss,
A celebration such as this,
So I tidied Roona's disarray,
And we continued on our way.

Should I tell or hold my tongue?
Clyde MacNeigh would have me hung,
For cowardly neglect of duty,
Surrendering his Holstein cutie,

To a fate far worse than death,
So I thought I'd save my breath.
The facts will some day come to light,
And not in pristine black and white.

But probably in red,
That day I'd face with mighty dread.
I'd better far be far away,
Beyond the reach of Clyde MacNeigh.

We entered von Kaye's wide demesne,
Awed and humbled by the scene,
A bearded seneschal bowed us in,
And welcomed us like long lost kin.

We were led to Hendrik's private suite,
Where he was munching Shredded Wheat,
He raised his head inquiringly,
Then turned away dismissively.

Looked down his nose, as if to say,
Cawn't you come another day?
He was the blasé dilettante,
Spurning our sweet debutante.

A dozen men then gathered round,
Scratched their heads and spat and frowned,
Debating whether push or pull,
Would motivate that reluctant bull.

If he don't do what he oughter,
He'll be a candidate for slaughter.
Poor Hendrik never saw the threat,
From expectations left unmet.

Then Roona felt she'd had enough,
Of this highfalutin' stuff,
She curled her lip as if she swore,
That she'd put up with nothing more,

Whirled around and tossed her head,
Vowing that she'd not be wed,
A sudden kick right to his brisket,
Persuaded Hendrik not to risk it.

The wedding guests, I now can laugh,
Scuttled off, like wind-blown chaff,
While Roona started on her way,
Heading home to *chez MacNeigh*.

She put on such a burst of speed,
There was no way that I could lead,
All that I could do was follow,
All the way to Howell's Hollow.

Where Brutus languished, still held fast,
Mulling o'er his checkered past,
And smiling at the memory,
Of chasing me up the big birch tree.

There I caught Roona's trailing rope,
And feeling that I now could cope,
Sat on a stump to think things through,
And consider what was best to do.

Roona showed great solicitude,
Toward that randy little dude,
She circled round and licked his nose,
And sniffed at him as at a rose,

And I myself could but admire,
That tough and spunky ball of fire,
No pampered prince nor grand marquis,
But just a guy like you or me.

I got the Princess home at last,
Watered, fed and penned up fast,
With her friends both young and old,
To whom her tale I'm sure she told.

I couldn't leave things as they were,
With lonely Brutus stuck out there,
There was absolutely no excuse,
I simply had to cut him loose.

It was near the close of day,
With Swedish saw, I made my way,
Back to Brutus and the tree,
And, in a jiffy, cut him free.

He stretched and yawned and staggered 'round,
Flexed his joints and, in a bound,
Charged again at me,
And chased me back up my tree.

He kept me there nigh till dawn,
Clutching the branch that I sat on.
Because I didn't sleep a wink,
It gave me lots of time to think.

I can tell what's short or long,
Far easier than what's right or wrong.
But guys like me don't need to sit,
Where bosses think we ought to fit,

MacNeigh considered Brutus junk,
But that ain't what ol' Brutus thunk.
I wonder if there mightn't be
A lesson there for guys like me.

When autumn came I took my pay,
And turned my back on Clyde MacNeigh.
I bummed around by road and rail,
And not till now ever told my tale.

On the morning of March 18, 1948, the body of Lancelot McDough was discovered on the grounds of the Transylvanian Hall about six miles west of Banshee. Clothing was in tatters and his face and body bore the marks of a savage beating, with cuts and possible stab wounds. As there had been a wedding dance in the hall on the previous night, the explanation that came most readily to mind was that McDough had fallen victim to the violence that was normally a part of social events at that location — most of it attributed to vampires or werewolves. It was an explanation that appeared to satisfy Officialdom. There was an inquest and a verdict that Lance had met his death at the hands of persons unknown. After a cursory investigation, the matter was quietly swept under a rug.

Officialdom might have been satisfied, but there were many in Banshee who were not. Among them was Edwina

Topdrawer-Wideacre, who knew she would feel Lance's absence more acutely than anyone else. Having been in Moose Jaw to be fitted with new dentures, she was absent from Banshee for the days immediately preceding and following the tragedy. She returned to Banshee only in time to view Lance's mortal remains laid out ready for burial. She quietly resolved to dig her way to the bottom of the affair.

She knew that Lance had been invited to sing at a St. Patrick's Day tea sponsored by the I.O.D.E. Lance had a fine tenor voice and was regularly called upon to perform at events of this nature. Prior to leaving for Moose Jaw, Edwina had been in close daily touch with Lance and knew that he intended to sing two or three sentimental Irish ballads. Word on the street was that he had appeared at the tea and had sung, but had not been seen since. The I.O.D.E. members all pleaded ignorance.

Something about their demeanor made Edwina suspect the imperial daughters were neither as ignorant nor as innocent as they pretended. She was determined to find out the truth. To that end she bought a bottle of the forty-cent sherry from the Government Liquor Store and invited Beth Diddley, the most malleable of her suspects, to tea. Before the sherry was half gone, Edwina knew everything.

Lance had come to the tea as expected. He circulated among those present, admired the decorations which made extensive use of shamrocks, the colour green and leprechauns, ate an egg salad sandwich, drank two cups of tea and, as was his wont, made himself agreeable to the ladies.

He was to be introduced to the gathering by Mrs. Esme Gossamer, who was the chief architect of the afternoon's proceedings. In her introductory remarks, a beaming Mrs.

Gossamer assured everyone that the proceeds from the tea would be put toward a very worthy cause. They would be sent home to England to help restore order among the Irish.

Mrs. Gossamer had blundered. She should have known that Lance had become an ardent Irish nationalist. Everyone else in town knew that. When Edwina heard what Mrs. Gossamer had said, she took a sharp breath and waited for what came next. She knew that Lance was also a fierce anti-imperialist. In the cartons stored in her back bedroom, she had several hand-drawn world maps whereon Lance had incurred the displeasure of his teachers by colouring the whole of the British Empire in black. This he had done, he told her, out of respect and sympathy for those brave folk who had died defending their homes against the British invaders.

Edwina sighed. She understood how Lance must have felt seeing Irish symbols and folklore being exploited for the continued subjugation of the Irish themselves. With Mrs. Gossamer's announcement, there was a sudden change in Lance's demeanor. He wouldn't put up with this. He strode over to the piano and spoke briefly to the pianist who had been his accompanist since he was a boy. She looked a little surprised, shrugged, tinkled with the keys for a few seconds and then moved into the introductory bars to "There'll Always Be An England."

That was what Lance sang, except that, wherever the words *England* or *English* were supposed to occur, he substituted *Ireland* and *Irish*. His performance was received with perfunctory applause from an audience more engaged with their egg salad sandwiches than with the lyrics of an over-familiar song. Lance savagely demolished another sandwich along with some pickled onions and tossed back another cup of tea. He was going to force a confrontation with the Organizing Committee.

When it came, it was hopeless. Try as he might, Lance could not make the Organizing Committee see the irony in their wanting to deny the Irish a sovereign and united homeland when they held that very concept so dear for themselves. He cursed them roundly for being so blindly self-righteous. The Organizing Committee would not hear. Instead, they swarmed him.

In five minutes Lance was dead. He had been stabbed several times with a butter knife, gouged with pointed toes and sharp heels, clawed, mauled and garroted with his own St. Patrick's Day necktie, the one decorated with tiny shillelaghs.

When they realized what they had done, the imperial daughters acted quickly to shift responsibility to someone else, the most plausible candidates being the notoriously violent members of the Transylvanian community. It was their good fortune that Vice-Chair Tilly Frumple had driven herself in from the farm with the family's pickup truck instead of the car. It was agreed that Tilly would drop the corpse off at the Transylvanian Hall as she passed it on her way home. They wrapped what was left of Lance in a tablecloth, put it in the truck and washed their hands of the whole affair.

Edwina knew that she would never get any co-operation from Officialdom in trying to expose the guilty or bring them to justice. She decided to do it herself. Over the next several months, membership in the Banshee Chapter of the I.O.D.E. was sharply reduced by a series of unexpected deaths. Food poisoning, falls, drowning, electrocution, asphyxiation and fire all took their toll. There were anxious whispers about the

Curse of Count Dracula. Chapter membership fell to only a few furtive souls who were constantly looking over their shoulders and adamantly refusing to accept executive positions.

During this time, the hours were not as empty for Edwina as one might have expected. She had an abundance of company. Her companions were a collection of voodoo dolls, each one resembling an individual from the Organizing Committee and each one bearing evidence of extreme trauma, one having been burned, another pierced with rusty nails and a third's stomach cavity filled with snippets of barbed wire.

The full poetic legacy of Lance McDough is yet to be determined. Publication of the bulk of his work is still a decade away. By then, popular thought might have advanced to the point where Lance was seventy-five years ago. In the meantime, the honour of discovering this genius and bringing him to public attention will not go to Professor Ergot. It is an honour that this author claims for himself.

Me and Charlie and the Concentrated Ground *

I guess me and Charlie dug most of the graves in this here cemetery. But I don't dig many now. They ain't so many buried out here no more and since Pete Branser got that backhoe, he digs most of 'em if he ain't busy on a job somewheres. That's why he ain't diggin' this grave here. He's away down to Cranberry Flats puttin' in a sewage system for that fella on the ranch along the river there. Big fella with a loud laugh. I seen him lots of times, but his name just slips me.

Yeah. Yeah. Holfeld. That's it. Well, I still get a grave to dig ever' so often, but I ain't so fussy about it no more. It was okay when Charlie was along, but he's layin' over there for quite awhile now. Six years last May since he died. I dug his grave all by myself. You know, me and Charlie useta joke about it. About which one of us would be diggin' the other one's grave, I mean. Guess I won, but I don't get no pleasure out of it.

*Previously published in the *Wascana Review*.

His grave is further down the slope, but you can see it from here all right. It's only got a wooden marker on it. Just past that one with the row of tin cans on it. Them cans had plants growin' in 'em once, but they all dried up and the cans is all rusted. Harry Blackthorne's missus put 'em there just before they moved out. That's where their oldest boy is. Got took with appendix durin' one January cold spell. Forty below and snow drifts was ten, twelve feet deep in places. Harry and his missus is livin' out in BC now. Their other boy was killed in the war. It's their place that Johnny Mason is farmin' now.

The oldest one is dated eighteen ninety-eight and that makes her easy the oldest cemetery in these parts. You see, they was homesteaders in here long before they was a province of Saskatchewan, and they had to have 'em a church, so they built one out here. They was no towns around here then. Ridpath didn't get started until the railroad come through here in eleven. The church stood right over there in the corner till they moved it into Ridpath and built onto it in there.

So this is by rights an Anglican churchyard and this is concentrated ground we're diggin'. It's all wrote down in the parish records. They's a map too of the whole cemetery showin' all the plots and some other papers what says how one of the bishops came up here in the early days from Regina or someplace to say his prayers and he concentrated the whole kaboodle — church and grounds — the cemetery and everything.

So she's concentrated all right. But she ain't no different to dig through. Me and Charlie done lots of diggin'. Cisterns and wells and cesspools and we know what the ground is like all through this country. This here ain't bad for diggin' right now, bein' it's a wet year, but it's a real bugger when it's bin dry for a long spell. And she's like cement when she's froze. Just hand me that pickaxe for a sec willya?

Charlie was real good to have on a job. Real smart fella and not scared to bend his back neither. Work sure went good when Charlie was in on it. He liked his booze more'n some mebbe, but that was his business, and it didn't make him no worse than some who never touch a drop. Fella couldn't want no better friend than Charlie.

That big one right along the fence? Yeah, she's some headstone all right. A real dandy. Me and Charlie set that one up for Eliot Windthorst. It came all the way from Winnipeg and it cost him a pile of money. Mebbe five–six hundred. But I guess a few hundred didn't hurt Eliot none. He likely figgered his wife wouldn't stay down if she didn't have the biggest stone in the cemetery.

Oh Eliot was well fixed all right. His hardware made money in the early days and he's hung onto it. He ain't never had to pinch. Not him. Always did drive a big car and kept help in the house for his wife too. The girls they had would never stay long though, 'cause his missus was always real hard to work for. Awful hard. The girls was always pickin' up and leavin' — except only one. One thing about diggin' here is that they ain't many rocks. They's places we would have throwed out a dozen by now. Big ones too.

Where? Yeah. That's a grave all right. Me and Charlie dug that one too. A girl from back in the hills is buried there. One of Miz Windthorst's girls. Blondest girl I ever seen. Couldn't of bin more'n seventeen when she came to work for Miz Windthorst, and that was a long time ago now. Her hair was sorta thin and real white. Just like a dandelion gone to seed. Finns, her people were and they farmed back there in the Paswegin Hills someplace. Lots of Finns back in there. A big settlement. Lucky buggers some o' them. Always got some rain, even in a dry year. Fifteen–twenty bushel crop when nobody else didn't even get his seed back. But they ain't all rich. Some o' them is just scratchin' away, as bad off as anybody else.

Yeah, they's lots o' them fair skinned and white headed, but this girl, Lempi was unusual so. Could of bin good lookin' enough, but a little too pale for most. Myself, I like 'em with a little more colour. And then, besides, she had that birthmark.

Bad enough, I guess. A big red splotch about the size of your hand. It came from about here down to the corner of her mouth, and then down like this to just under her jaw. You couldn't see it from one side and she'd look pretty nice till she turned her head and that would give you a start unless you was used to it. But she was real quiet and a good worker. They say she did all the housework for Miz Windthorst while she was there.

Miz Windthorst, you know, was a pretty busy woman. You know the kind. Eliot ran his business and the town council and his missus ran ever'thing else in town.

She was real quiet, this Lempi was. Sort of 'shamed I guess about that birthmark and she didn't go out hardly at all. And that was the way Miz Windthorst wanted it. To church on a Sunday night mebbe, and that was about it. You see, she prob'ly didn't talk nothin' but Finn until she started school likely. They's all Finns back in there through them hills and in those days none of 'em would of talked much else. Her English was sort of broken like. None of the young fellas took any interest in her and she didn't encourage 'em none.

It must of bin pretty lonesome for her I guess. She got sort of cut off from her own people too. Her mother had died and the dad lost his homestead after that. Then he went away to Ontario to work in the bush. Lots o' them Finns is bush workers. Cut pulpwood and stuff like that.

Lempi? Oh she stayed on at Windthorsts for a long time. Ten years anyways I guess. Don't think she went out with a fella even once in all that time. So it was a real su'prise when she got married, specially all at once like she did. What's that? No. Not Lempi. They was nobody messin' around with her.

A funny thing, you know. It was in pretty hard times and they was lots of tramps on the move. Young fellas ridin' the rods and folks got used to 'em so's they didn't pay 'em much attention. But that didn't stop half the women in town from gettin' high-sterical when this fella showed up. He was wanderin' around the streets and lookin' at houses and starin' at any women who was out in their yard. Nobody saw him blow in. Guess he must of hiked in or maybe got off of a freight or somethin'.

He didn't do nothin' but just walked around the streets gawkin'. The women folks was buzzin' and gagglin' over him and callin' their kids in off the street and finally, Miz Windthorst made Eliot phone the Mounties over at Poplar Lake. The police didn't come or nothin'. The corp'ral told Eliot that there wasn't no escaped convicts loose that he knew of and he wasn't goin' to drive no thirty-six miles to interdoose him to no tramp.

I'll say he didn't. Eliot was awful close-mouthed, and he wouldn't tell nothin' on hisself anyways. Mabel Gordon — that's Harry Gordon's missus — Mabel Watson she was then — she was workin' in the telephone office and she heard it all ... She don't work there no more, 'cept unless somebody's took sick or somethin'. But she sure didn't keep no official secrets as well as she might of while she was on the switchboard, let me tell you. Real good operator though. She could put you through to Saskatoon or Regina in just a few minutes. Almost as fast as you could think about it.

After awhile this fella went over and sat by the side of the Pool elevator. He just sat there. A few times he'd get up and hike down the track a ways in one direction or the other, but not far, and he always come back to the elevator. I'll bet if Miz Windthorst had of knew what was goin' to happen she would of done somethin' more to try to run him outta town. She didn't know though, and when she found out, it was too late.

It was the kids who was most curious. Guess, besides, they was a little bolder than the older folks. Anyway, some boys crossed over the tracks to talk to this fella. Turned out he was just ordinary and there was nothin' suspicious about him at all. It was near supper time and he had took his pack out from a pile of ties where he had stashed it away when he first come. The pack was open and he was havin' something to eat. A hunk of bread the kids said and a sausage as big as his boot that he was chewin' on and a tin can that he had filled with water from the CNR pump. Bygod, that reminds me I'm thirsty. We better try what's in that mickey.

They say age improves it, but I think this stuff must be growed up by now. Makes the world more cheerful don't it? It's pretty fair brew, but it ain't nothing like what Charlie useta make. They'd drive all the way over from Poplar Lake to buy his stuff. He sure ran a good still. Me and Charlie sure drank a pile of it and we buried quite a few empties out here, let me tell you. You'd be surprised at the strait-laced old ladies what's gut an empty bottle tucked in with 'em. I stuck a full one in behind Charlie's rough box. The old bugger woke up thirsty more often than not.

But he would of done the same for me. They was lots of times he left me the tag end of a bottle and told me to keep her till morning.

Yeah. The kids tried talking to this fella, but they couldn't get very far. He couldn't talk much English. A few words, you know, but real broken like and hard to understand. But they was there for awhile talkin' away, with the kids mebbe mockin' him and gettin' a little sassy. And then Pete Rychenko showed up. Pete was the section foreman here then and he was on his way home for supper. He seen these kids and went over to see what was goin' on. Well, it turned out that him and this fella talked the same whatever-it-is kind of jabbersloovian lingo, and the first thing you know, this guy was jabberin' away for all he was worth.

Well, Pete took him along home with him. Him and his big pack. And I guess it wasn't long before Pete knew all about him. Hell, the whole town knew all about him before the supper dishes was done.

You know, I think you better take a little bit outta that corner there. She's gettin' a little outta square.

Them Rychenko kids could hardly have et their supper before they was over town tellin' their friends. It went just like a prairie fire. Ever' one was tellin' ever'one else that this tramp had come to marry Lempi.

You bet that's right. He figgered on gettin' married. It seems they got to writin' to each other somehow, through a magazine mebbe or some kind of lonely hearts club. He must of had somebody put his letters into English for him and read Lempi's letters too I s'pose. Anyways, he had decided it was time to come and see her and make his offer face to face.

Guess Lempi was just about the last person in town to find out that he was here. Miz Windthorst was real mortified. Someone had run over right off to tell her so she knew what was up. Likely she seen that she might lose the only hired girl she ever had who'd take all the dirt she dished out and not kick back. She stomped and scuttled around as cross as a mink with young'uns and then she lit into Lempi. I guess she ripped into her up and down and crossways. My missus happened to be over there. She had scrubbed out the church and had went over to Miz Windthorst to get paid. She heard a lot of what Miz Windthorst said. Lempi wasn't sayin' much, but she wasn't exactly runnin' scared neither.

Well, it wasn't long before the fella — Nick his name was — showed up at Windthorst's house askin' for Lempi. Rychenko must of told him where Lempi lived. Pretty well ever'body in town knew that Miz Windthorst wouldn't like this fella comin' round there, but Rychenko and his missus wouldn't care nothin' about that. His wife was a big stout woman who was all day hoein' her cabbages or splittin' ties for firewood. She sure as hell didn't worry none about Miz Windthorst and her hoity-toity crew. No garlic snapper like her would ever of got invited to one of their tea parties anyways.

Let's have another pull from that bottle. This diggin' don't get no easier.

Anyways, Miz Windthorst wouldn't let this Nick fella inta the house when he got there, and she told Lempi that if she wanted to talk to him she'd hafta do it outside. So Lempi couldn't do nothin' else but go outside with him. They walked around the block a couple o' times but they had half the people in town out on the streets to have a look at 'em, so they went down to the railroad and walked up and down the tracks almost until dark.

That was all it took. They decided to get hitched.

No. No. He wasn't no tramp at all. Ever'body figgered at first that he was, but he wasn't. He'd bin in Canada for two–three years workin' on a railroad extra gang. Savin' his money. Y'see, he was a shoemaker by trade and he figgered to get hisself a shoe repair shop. A wife who could talk English would be a big help to him. I dunno how he explained his proposition to her, but it must of sounded all right to Lempi 'cause she took him up on it.

About nine o'clock, she went back to Windthorsts and told 'em she was gettin' hitched. Miz Windthorst just laughed at her at first. She acted as if it was just a joke. Like I said, Lempi didn't have no friends and nobody took 'em serious at all.

Me and Charlie wasn't no better than nobody else. Maybe we was worse. We hee-hawed and cracked just as many jokes as the next fella. That Charlie was real comical if he wanted to be. Just let him get to feelin' good and there was no stoppin' him. Real light on his feet too. Nobody could touch him at either dancin' or fightin'. Real smooth he was. Exceptional so for such a big man.

But me and Charlie was just havin' fun. We didn't mean no harm. Not like some.

Miz Windthorst got pretty miserable and tried to raise all the hell she could to try to make Lempi change her mind. But Lempi showed more dang spunk than anyone ever figgered she had and she wouldn't give in to nothin' Miz Windthorst said. Guess Miz Windthorst stewed and badgered at her all the next day, but Lempi stuck right to her guns. Then, when Miz Windthorst seen she couldn't make Lempi change her mind, she kicked her out. Paid her off and kicked her out right then and there. Said she was a disgrace and that there was no place for her under a respectable roof.

Well, Lempi packed what little she had and moved down to the hotel. And it was a pretty rough place that old Bill Griffin was runnin' in them days. No place for a girl to stay at all.

Things was movin' a mite too fast for Nick, of course. He didn't know nothin' about this country you know. Green as grass and Lempi was just about as bad. Most folks was laughin' and jokin' about 'em and some was even tryin' to pull their leg. Some was worse than others. They'd sit around in the beer parlour and get lots of bright ideas. You know how it is.

You figger on savin' that tiger's milk for another day?

Well, they couldn't get hitched in Ridpath right away anyways. The Anglican preacher, Wilding, was away on holidays. They was away back east visitin' his wife's folks and they wasn't no other preacher right around here. So they didn't know what to do and nobody was bein' very helpful neither. They was all too busy laughin'. Even me and Charlie.

I guess though, if we had of knew what them fellas was up to, we wouldn't have let them do it. But they kept the dirty part of their plan secret, and they fooled ever'one. They was sure set on provin' how smart they was.

It was Bill Wentworth and George Alworthy. Wentworth was one o' them goddam remittance men. His folks in

England was rich and they sent him money regular just so's he'd stay away. Them two never showed their faces around here for a long time after it was all over let me tell you. Just once was all. And then Charlie tackled 'em both. Offered to lick 'em both — either separate or both together. They knew he could do it too. Charlie useta pick up a curlin' rock with one hand and turn it over to look at the bottom. If it needed cleanin', he'd just rub it on his chest, sorta absent-minded like, as if that curlin rock didn't weigh no more 'n his mitts. I sure did like to see him do that.

Them bastards really planned it out. They made Lempi and Nick believe that they was tryin' to help and they drove 'em to Saskatoon so's they could get hitched up there right away that day. And you know they put on a mock weddin' just to fool those two. They rounded up some of their pals and got one of them to pertend to be the preacher and they made Nick and Lempi think that they was hitched all legal and proper. They had even printed up a phony certificate — a kind of a jokin' one it was. Nick showed it to me afterward. They sure did it up brown let me tell you. Then they put 'em on the afternoon train and sent 'em back to Ridpath.

Oh they fooled ever'body all right. While they was gone, Mabel Gordon, that's Harry Gordon's wife — Mabel Watson she was then — got the notion of havin' them a party. So she got to phonin' and makin' arrangements. She's pretty good-hearted even if she ain't too good at keepin' secrets, and she likes a good time too. Anyways they hadn't bin a dance in town in quite a long while. So she got this party goin'. They was a bunch met 'em at the train that night and took 'em over to the hall and they was dancin' and so on. Gents paid two bits to pay the hall rent and the ladies brought lunch.

Whoever had a fiddle or a accordeen brought it along and played for free. They was a lot of people there considerin' that some of the womenfolk didn't want to get on the bad side of Miz Windthorst. It wasn't no big splash, mind you, but they was lots o' young folks. They took up a collection and got a few dollars to give 'em. They wasn't many of the high mucky mucks there, but you could tell that nobody ever had a better party. And Nick and Lempi was real su'prised. I don't s'pose that either of them had ever had any kind of party before and they was sure tickled. It's too bad it all ended the way it did. Ever'thin' looked there for awhile as if it could go real good for 'em.

No. They didn't go away. They stayed right there in Ridpath. Like I said, this Nick was a shoemaker. He had a little money saved up — Lempi mighta had some too I guess — and they was gonna set up shop somewheres. Well, they was a vacant store building right there on the main street. It's burned down now, but it had stood empty for two, three years, ever since Chet Nelson went broke in 'er. Livin' quarters upstairs. All she needed was cleanin' out and a little fixin' up. And the districk sure needed a shoemaker. Farmers was still usin' lots of horses in them days and they had lots of harness to repair. Harness and binder canvas, besides all the shoes. Lots of work to keep a shoemaker real busy.

Y'know, ever'body 'cept Miz Windthorst and her crew got to singin' a differ'nt tune. People started pitchin' in to help. Mebbe some was doin' it just to spite Miz Windthorst who hadn't bin able to get another hired girl and was still pretty well up in the air about it. But it wasn't long until Nick and Lempi was settled right in. It was easy done. In them days you didn't need much to start out. A bed, a table and a stove.

Not like now. Young folks now figger they got to start out at where their old folks left off.

They had threw a pa'tition across the big front room. Nick's workshop was in back, and the front they had fixed up real slick. They had some boots and fancy bridles and even a saddle. Stuff all for sale. Pompoms and other things for decoratin' up a team of horses. And all neat and orderly just like a reg'lar store — not a dang scrummage o' junk like most shoemaker shops.

They started doin' real good in there too, considerin' ever'thing. O'course in them times, most folks couldn't afford to buy new stuff. It seems that fix and mend was all that anybody ever did. Nick was real busy. They was both busy 'cause Lempi spent as much time in the shop as Nick did. He'd do the hard stuff that took a real shoemaker and she'd clean and polish and help anywhere she could.

Lempi mebbe wasn't no shoemaker, but she sure helped to draw the trade. The day they started business, they stuck a pair of Charlie's old boots in the window. Right there out in front. Old boots they was. One was so twisted and chewed up and worn out you'da thought it had gone through a thrashin' machine. The other was all fixed up. New half-sole. New heel. Stitched the uppers all up. All oiled and polished. Then laced 'er up partway with new rawhide laces. She looked as good as new. And right beside it sat the other one lookin' like it belonged on the trash heap. That was Lempi's idea. She had a head on her, let me tell you. And she didn't seem to give a damn no more about that birthmark. She acted just like she had forgot she had it.

I'll say somethin' happened. It sure did. When it blew up, it blew up all at once, and then it was all over. It was mostly

Miz Windthorst's fault. And o'course Wentworth and Allworthy. But I s'pose ever'body was some to blame. Or if she'd of had someone ... But sometimes people don't make no kind of sense at all.

Y'see, I s'pose it was bound to happen that word would get out that there hadn't been no real weddin'. It got whispered around town, but nobody was up to tellin' Nick or Lempi. And with the first bit o' talk, Miz Windthorst made it her business to find out. So o'course she found out that there hadn't been no licence issued and there wasn't no record of such a weddin'. That was all it took.

Miss Windthorst got all dressed up one afternoon — Friday it was, just before train time — all dressed up with her white gloves on and collected a couple of her fat-assed sidekicks and they went marchin' in to Nick and Lempi's place. Lempi was there alone. Nick had gone to the train station to pick up some express. So Lempi was there like she usually was and Miz Windthorst just ripped into her all over again, only worse. Told her that she was a stupid blockhead and that she was livin' in sin but wasn't foolin' nobody. That she was just a joke and that the whole town was laughin' at her. It took Lempi a little while to get the whole drift of what they was sayin', but I guess them women wasn't shy of helpin' her to understand.

When fine'ly Lempi unnerstood what all they was gettin' at, she took it awful hard. She broke right down and ran upstairs to hide. Y'see she believed the whole town was in on the joke and that she was a reg'lar laughin' stock. She wouldn't talk to nobody, she was so ashamed. I guess all she could think of was to get away anyway she could. Trouble was, there was no place for her to go.

So she took gopher poison. Fulla strick-nyne that stuff. Throws ya inta convulsions. They say she was awful sick before she died.

Pretty well the whole town was squabblin' over her funeral. Youda thought Miz Windthorst would of bin satisfied, but she wasn't, not even then. It was about a burial place you see. Miz Windthorst claimed that the cemetery was concentrated ground and that it's never allowed that no suicide should be buried in concentrated ground. So me and Charlie got instructions to dig Lempi's grave outside the fence. Right alongside was okay, but it had to be on the other side.

Me and Charlie just couldn't see that. 'Specially Charlie. He spoke right out agin it. He figgered the town had done her enough wrong without doin' that besides. He felt real sorry about it and so did I, but they had give us our orders.

I guess though, in the end, me and Charlie did the best we could. We didn't know what to do at first, so we got out the plan of the cemetery to see how many feet we had to the road allowance. And we looked up to see who was buried where so Lempi wouldn't have to lie beside some mean-tempered old bat. Then Charlie saw what to do. And as soon as he explained it to me, I didn't need no coaxin'.

Folks figgered we was awful slow diggin' Lempi's grave. We barely had it ready before it was time to use it. Y'see nobody knew that we had worked right through the night movin' that dang fence around the cemetery. We spread the dirt from the postholes so's it wouldn't be noticed and we piled the tumbleweed agin the fence just like it was before.

Y'see, along the south side there where Lempi is buried,

we moved the fence in a few feet. And along the north side there, we moved 'er a few feet out.

Yep. Lempi is layin' outside the fence, but she's still in concentrated ground. And up there at the north end, Miz Windthorst is inside the fence, but she ain't in no concentrated ground. She's really in Baldy Wickup's pasture. And Baldy never gave it no blessin'. They's some alkali through there and it don't hardly grow enough grass for a billygoat. Just foxtail.

Looks like this is another dead soldier. Guess we can throw away the cork.

Burning Bridges

Although Fay and Sam Hobb had been married for thirty-four years, they were still excessively fond of each other. She looked to him for guidance in all matters pertaining to electricity, plumbing and internal combustion engines, while he acknowledged her authority in everything that had to do with diet and domestic décor. With there being nothing left on which they might possibly disagree, their days and nights were filled with adoring looks, whispered endearments and loving embraces.

Their union had not been blessed with progeny — not for a want of procreative activity on their part, but simply because the stork had not seen fit to call. The Hobbs had thus allowed themselves to become completely immersed in each other and in their respective careers (she was a librarian, and he a biologist). Now, for the third time since their marriage, they were burning their bridges behind them. The first time was when they resigned from their positions in Yorkshire's

East Pookington, sold their meager household effects and sailed for Canada. In Canada, their rich Yorkshire accents turned out to be neither the social nor the professional handicap they had been in England, and the two of them advanced rapidly in their respective fields of endeavour. In ten short years, she became the Chief Librarian in a thriving prairie metropolis, while he was chairing the Biology Department of the provincial university and had become recognized as an authority on toadstools, mushrooms and other flora of that same anemic persuasion.

During their tenure in their chosen city, they prospered exceedingly. They moved several times, starting from relatively modest accommodations and progressing to domiciles of ever increasing splendour, making a tidy profit with each move. They invested shrewdly and accumulated pensions the way less astute couples accumulate debts. They became wealthy far beyond their youthful expectations.

Upon retirement, hoping to escape the rigours of another long succession of prairie winters, they burned their second set of bridges by moving to Victoria, a city reputed to be even more English than England itself. There, those same humble Yorkshire accents now proved to be an impediment to their acceptance into Victoria's impermeable upper crust. Neither of the Hobbs was completely sufficient unto the other. They were both unhappy. They sold their new oceanfront villa at a handsome profit and prepared to burn their third set of bridges.

First, they arranged with their solicitors — the firm of Wimpole, Walpole and Freep — to receive the income from their mortgages, stocks, bonds, pensions and whatnot and hold it until they had settled at a new address. Then, the law firm was to forward to them, month by month, their income as it came pouring in from its manifold points of origin.

Next, while shopping for a new car with which to leave Victoria in a style commensurate with the disdain they now felt for the city, they spotted a mammoth motorhome languishing on a used car lot. It had been briefly owned by a rising rock star who had succumbed to one or another of the many excesses to which rising rock stars seem peculiarly susceptible. It was a state-of-the-art vehicle with every conceivable electronic communication and recording device computerized, automated and seamlessly installed everywhere within the behemoth's burled walnut interior. The Hobbs bought it at a fraction of its original cost.

"We will drive," said Sam as he wheeled their new home south from Vancouver. "We will drive until we come to the perfect spot."

"And when we get there, we will know it immediately," asserted Fay.

"And we'll do just what we want to do," declared Sam, "and nothing more."

"Exactly," sighed Fay. "I'm going to write poetry. Delicate little poems. Odes and triolets. And haikus."

"And I'll illustrate them. In watercolours." Sam had added to his reputation and his bank account by doing the illustrations himself for his bestseller, *A Field Guide to Edible Wild Fungi*. "We could make our own books. Elegant little volumes of your poems."

"Oh, Sam! *Exquisite* little volumes! Beautifully bound in silk. Or calf."

"Or birchbark. Or snakeskin," suggested Sam, who rather fancied himself an outdoorsman. "And we'll place them in fashionable little boutiques."

"Oh yes! In New York and London. That would be wonderful. On display in charming little boutiques. And art galleries. Not shelved in some old barn of a bookstore." They lost themselves in joyful speculation.

Meanwhile, back in Victoria, a completely different agenda was being planned for them. At a secluded table in a once posh bistro, a fussily dressed woman was huddled in close conversation with her escort. Modern chemistry and artful camouflage, to the advantage of both, had concealed the onset of wrinkles, greying hair and expanding waist-lines. Affecting a need to hear her companion the better, she hitched her chair even closer. He stroked a finely sculpted moustache and smiled indulgently, displaying as dazzling a set of dentures as Corrections Canada had ever fashioned for a long-term guest. "We can't talk here," he murmured. "Let's go to your apartment."

With the twitch of an imperious eyebrow, he summoned the waitress and settled the bill, pointedly writing in a lavish gratuity, all done with lordly aplomb and a stolen credit card. Everything that might later have ensued at the lady's apartment is not important to this narrative. Suffice it to say that they discussed in detail how to steal the identities along with the assets of Fay and Sam Hobb.

She was Willa Burk, during the week, the trusted human dynamo who masterminded the daily operations of Wimpole, Walpole and Freep, and the very one who selected Fay and Sam Hobb as ideal targets for identity theft. Outside of office hours, she had allowed herself to become just another foolish old maid who was prepared to risk everything in a last desperate lunge at marital bliss. There is no need to say more about her companion except that his alias at the time was

Fitzroy Earl, and he was a man of infinite criminal resource. He had surreptitiously fixed to the motorhome a homing device that enabled him to track the Hobbs wherever they might drive. He had already spent several weeks preparing for a new persona, forging identification and buying personal items bearing the monogram he aspired to make his own. He decided against making similar provision for Miss Burk. Good forgeries are expensive.

The plan was for Miss Burk to take her vacation reasonably coincidental with their intended victims' departure from Victoria. Then the wolves would follow the lambs, seizing any opportunity along the way to pretend to make friends, the better to lure them to a place private enough for a double murder. At the end of her vacation period, Miss Burk would return to her duties at Wimpole, Walpole and Freep and do all that was necessary to divert everything owned by the Hobbs to her partner at whatever place they had chosen to begin their new life together.

Two weeks into Miss Burk's vacation, everything was going according to plan.

The wolves had befriended the lambs so successfully that the two couples had agreed to spend a few nights camping in the wilderness. But now, the time had come to end the pretence. The palatial motorhome was just a speck in the vast Arizona desert with Earl's stolen minivan a smaller speck beside it. They were screened from the distant highway by a conveniently placed cluster of scraggly trees.

Fay and Sam, equipped with cameras and specimen boxes, had spent the morning among the trees looking for fungi. When they returned to the motorhome shortly before noon, they had several fine specimens of mushroom. "I'll have to check them out," Sam told Fay. "Whether catalogued or not, they do look delicious." As they passed between the motorhome and the minivan, they came across Earl who was putting the finishing touches to an oblong pit that he had just dug. "My goodness! What a deep hole!" exclaimed Fay. "We didn't know you were planning anything like that."

"Such a deep pit really isn't necessary," remonstrated Sam. "We will have so little garbage to dispose of. Vegetable waste could just be left exposed on the ground. The bugs and scorpions would devour it in a day. And the paper and glass we planned to drop off where it can be recycled. But this was a lot of work. I should have helped you with it."

Earl flashed his brilliant dentures. "You can help fill it." And he cackled gleefully in appreciation of his private joke.

"We found some very fine mushrooms. It will take me half an hour to enter them in my notes, but if you can come over about noon, we'll share them for lunch." It was so agreed.

When the guests arrived for lunch, Earl had an automatic pistol tucked in his waistband. Fay couldn't contain her surprise. "What on earth are you going to do with that gun?" She favoured banning all firearms from existence.

"We're sorry, but we can't put off telling you any longer. We're going to shoot you — to death of course — and we're going to do it now." Earl couldn't resist putting on a bit of the class he had gained from watching movies. "I am, of course, truly sorry."

"But why?" asked Sam. "What did we ever do to you?"

"Not a thing. You have been nothing but kindness itself. But it's like this." And Earl went on to explain the *raison d'être* behind their arriving for lunch armed with an automatic.

Fay assessed the situation. "Very well. You have a gun and

we don't. That seems to put you in charge. But Sam and I have lived a quiet and orderly life. We don't want our final moments to be all screams and bullets and bloodshed. For most of the morning we were looking forward to a pleasant lunch on these mushrooms. We have a bottle of Chablis in the cooler and some fine Camembert. We would like our last meal to be a festive one with the friends we thought you to be. Could we delay the execution while I whip up something with these mushrooms — perhaps a quiche? If you agree, our invitation to lunch still stands."

It was a bizarre notion — but both Earl and Miss Burk found it romantic and incredibly appealing. Miss Burk positively shivered with delight. This *would* be a meal to remember! They smiled their acceptance and lent themselves assiduously to their roles as honoured guests. Earl playfully waggled a forefinger at Fay. "Now don't think for a moment that I would fall for that old poisonous-mushroom gambit. It went out with the Borgias."

Sam spoke up indignantly, "Poisonous-mushroom gambit? Not in my house! Mushrooms are my life and I love them dearly. I will never use them as a tool for deception or for any ignoble purpose. Not even to save my life." Then he caught himself. "But I'm afraid I am speaking too vehemently. We want a little gaiety. Let me see if I can find some music." He stepped over to the sound system's control panel. It had a bewildering array of buttons, switches and dials. He pressed something at random and got the late lamented rock star. "Humph! I'll keep trying."

While Fay prepared lunch under the watchful eyes of her guests, Sam opened the wine. After the third round of toasts, he had to open a second bottle. Fay produced a green salad garnished with bright red berries plucked from a desert shrub growing outside their door. "These berries have such a piquant flavour," she said. "If I eat one, I have to eat a dozen." She popped one in her mouth. Sam kept fiddling with buttons, switches and dials.

The salad was eaten and the bowls set aside. The quiche was next. Sam pressed another button and the room was filled with Earl's voice. He seemed to be talking on a telephone. "... *Yeah, sweetie, I really want to dump the ugly old cow and bury her with the others, but I'm going to need her for a week or two back in Victoria, just to wind things up. You just sit tight, honey, there in Vegas, and when everything is set, you can join me in Mexico. And keep practising to be Mrs. Hobb ...*"

Sam was peering into a miniature window in the control panel. "It says here that this call was recorded yesterday and was transmitted to everyone in my address book. That includes Wimpole, Walpole and Freep. So I'm afraid your game is up."

"So it is," agreed Earl. "But no crime has yet been committed. So let's just finish lunch and go our separate ways. And no hard feelings, eh old chap?"

"That's up to you. You see, there's a problem with the salad garnish. Around here, those little red berries are called 'flamethrowers.' As soon as your digestive enzymes dissolve their waxy coating, your entire stomach cavity will seem to catch fire and you will die in extreme agony. You saw Fay eat one? Look again. You will see that she is wearing only one of her bright red earrings.

"Miss Burk, I believe you will most certainly have burned the bridge that leads back to Wimpole, Walpole and Freep. Dear me! You look as if you are about to have smoke come swirling out of your ears."

Epitaph for
Moses Bearskin

Moses Bearskin was dead. Someone had shot him. That was the first thing that Pa and Eddie heard upon their arrival in town. Moses was dead and his funeral would be at two-thirty right there in town in the Anglican Church. The church on the reserve had burned down in the winter so the Indians had to borrow the church in town for the funeral. That's why there were so many Indians in town. "The preacher better nail down the pews," Eddie heard someone say. "Them Indians will steal anything that's loose at both ends." But Eddie didn't think that anyone, not even an Indian, would steal from the church. Especially not at a funeral.

Whoever had shot Moses nobody knew for sure, or at least nobody was saying. It must have been an accident because nobody would shoot old Moses on purpose. Except maybe one of his women. People said that, for an Indian, Moses was pretty good. You could trust him at least some of the time, but not when it came to women. "He's got more women than a harrow has teeth. An' most o' them is married to someone else. Maybe someone decided that Bearskin was hangin' around his wigwam a little too close."

"Yeah, in his bare skin." The speaker guffawed in appreciation of his own wit.

"Well, them days is over for Moses. He's a good Indian now all right." Everyone laughed. "Yep, a good Indian is a dead Indian."

It had been the longest and the heaviest rain that Eddie had ever seen. It had started with a thunderstorm that had knocked out the telephone, which, Mama complained, still wasn't working. And now, after three sodden days, nothing could be done in the fields, so Pa had decided to go to town. "Get Duke and Daisy in from the pasture," he had told Eddie. "We better take the team and buggy. We could likely get through with the truck all right, but we'd tear the road up too bad." Eddie hurried to do as he was told. From what his father had said, he understood that he was expected to go along.

"Lucky for me it's summer holidays," he thought.

Mamma had chosen to stay home. "The bread is ready for the oven," she said. "And maybe with you two out from under my feet, I'll be able to get some work done. But you can take Ruthie with you. She'd like a trip to town."

Eddie was not impressed with that. Ruthie was only five and was so shy that she wanted to hold his hand all the time. It was embarrassing. If Ruthie stayed home, he would be free to run off with friends. With all this rain, there would surely be other farm boys in town. Maybe some from his own school, all looking for company. But Eddie knew there was no use in protesting. If he said anything, he'd be the one to stay home.

And now, in town, everyone was talking about Moses

Bearskin and how he had come to be shot. No one had seen him since Saturday morning and then, Monday afternoon, Joe Parker had come across his body in the yard of the old Winstead place. It was Joe who had phoned the police. Because of the muddy roads, the Mounties couldn't get out there with their car so Joe had to take them with his horse and buggy.

Then Joe had been called on to help Doc Murray with the autopsy. The creek had overflowed and washed out the highway so the doctor had to come from Longacre on the railway jigger. They had laid Moses out bare naked on a table in the back room of the old Wong Lee laundry and the doctor had cut him up to find out for sure what had killed him.

Eddie heard all this from some town boys. They acted so smart because they had so much to tell. Eddie wondered what the town boys would think if they knew that Moses had worked for his dad and had slept in their bunkhouse. He decided not to tell them.

Pa decided to go to the funeral so took Ruthie over to Auntie Barb's house for the afternoon. "Moses was a good friend," Pa said. Auntie Barb lived in town and didn't have any kids. She liked to fuss over Ruthie. That left Eddie free to stay downtown and listen to all the talk on the street. He wished he had heard it all first hand from Joe Parker himself and not from those town kids. They thought they were so smart.

But Eddie had known Moses for as long as he could remember. And now Moses was dead. Eddie tried to imagine what Moses would have looked like lying there on a table in the old Wong Lee laundry. He had heard of other people dying, but it was never anyone he knew and never of someone being shot dead. And now it had happened to Moses, someone who had eaten at their table and slept in their bunkhouse. He had been shot and left to die and be rained on in a weedy old farmyard. Who could have done such a thing?

"Prob'ly a bunch of them was havin' a whoop-up an' they got to fightin'. Likely nobody knows who did the shootin' or even who was there," a man was saying. "If we could just keep them in booze an' bullets for a few years, they'll settle the Indian problem all by theirselves."

Pa had often called on Moses when he needed help on the farm. He said that Moses knew more about horses than any dozen other people, white or Indian, all put together. "Moses ain't a bronco buster," Pa often said. "He don't break a horse. He educates it."

As soon as Daisy's colt was old enough, Moses was going to take her home to the reserve and train her for riding. "Maybe I should take Eddie too," Moses had said. "Then I could train horse and rider at the same time." Eddie was glad that Moses was only joking because he wouldn't want to go and stay on the reserve, not even for one day. The kids at school said that the Indians ate funny things like gophers and frogs — even snakes. And Mamma wouldn't think much of the idea either. She always worried about fleas and bedbugs whenever Moses was around. And besides, Eddie didn't think he needed to be taught how to ride a horse, at least not by some old Indian.

At harvest time, Pa always hired Moses for stooking and threshing. "Moses can use the cash," Pa said. Whenever he could, Eddie would go out to stook with Moses or, if it was threshing time, drive the horses while Moses pitched the sheaves onto the hayrack.

Whenever Moses was there for overnight, Mama would

not allow him to sleep in the house. Not even in winter. "He can sleep in the bunkhouse," she insisted. "We don't need any of those redskin fleas in here."

"In France," Pa said, "we was all lousy. The cooties that bit Moses came to him from a bunch of white guys, but I didn't hear him complain."

When the threshing crew came in for supper, Moses always sat at the foot of the table. He didn't ever use his plate the same as everyone else. When the gravy bowl got to him, he would keep it. Then, everything else that he wanted to eat — even his pie — just got dumped in with the gravy. Mamma learned that she'd have to have two gravy bowls, one for Moses and another for everyone else.

When he was young, Moses had gone to a residential school and had learned to read and write. His handwriting was the best that Eddie had ever seen. The words flowed so evenly across the page, with every letter perfectly formed. Even Mamma couldn't write like that. "You must have had good teachers," Eddie once said.

Moses didn't answer right away. He just twisted his mouth a bit and then sort of snorted before he said, "Oh yeah. They taught us Indian kids lots of stuff. Real good."

Pa would fill a big bucket with bottled beer and lower it down the well to cool. When the harvesters came in from the field, Eddie would help crank the bucket up from the well and bring the cold beer to the house where the men were washing up and waiting for their supper. Eddie had heard Mamma say that it was against the law to give beer to an Indian, but Moses was handed a bottle just the same as everyone else. "He gets thirsty too," said Pa. "Just don't say anything about it."

But Eddie knew that Moses got drunk sometimes. Last Christmas there was a special program in the church. It had just started and the people were singing carols, but it wasn't going so good because Sadie Metcalf was playing the organ. Sadie could play the piano well enough, but she had never had to play that persnickety old pump organ before and couldn't seem to get the hang of it. Then Moses stumbled in shouting, "Merry Christmas!" and wanting to shake hands with everybody. "I heard the singin'," he said, "an' I thought I'd come in an' sing with you. I like to sing." And then he started to sing. He sang louder and better than anyone else in the church. He knew the words to all the songs and he just sang until everybody joined in and sang along with him until the preacher said it was time for lunch.

Some people were mad because the program hadn't gone the way they had planned it, but others said it was the best Christmas program they had ever had. Sadie Metcalf said that Moses had saved her from the worst night of her life and she hoped he'd get drunk and come to church every Sunday. "Then we could chop up that wheezy old pump organ for firewood."

"Moses learned all them songs in school," Pa said, "and a church school at that. The preacher is lucky that Moses didn't sing the songs he learned in the army. He can still sing them too after he's had a couple of drinks. That would have been quite a program." Pa laughed at the thought.

"They say he was one hell of a soldier," a man was saying.

· "All them redskins are wild fighters," said another. "Bloody savages."

Eddie could hear more fragments of conversation. "He was in the infantry ... a regiment outa Regina ... went overseas with a bunch of local fellas ... got picked for a sniper ... all them Indians is crack shots ... Moses could shoot the balls off a horsefly from a quarter mile away ..."

The funeral service seemed to be over, for Eddie could see a stream of people leaving the church. Yet a large group remained, most of them clustered around a big red grain truck that Eddie recognized as one that Pa had traded in a year ago. Yes, there were people, all women it seemed, and all wearing shawls and kerchiefs, seated on benches in the truck box. Information spread along the sidewalk. "They want to bury him out on the reserve ... mourners and the coffin are all in that truck ... but they can't get the truck started ... they're gonna get a tow from Hunter's Garage."

A few minutes later, another large truck pulled up to stop in front of the first one. Two men got out to attach a chain from the rear of their truck to the front of the other. They got back in their own truck and pulled out into the muddy street towing the improvised hearse with its two rows of mourners seated along the sides. Only their heads and shoulders were visible above the high sides of the truck. Their kerchiefs and shawls gave them a sombre uniformity. "Just like crows sitting on a rail," Eddie heard someone say.

With motor racing and horn blaring, the strange cortege roared down the street. The windows in the lead truck were open, through which the driver and passenger both waved as they passed by knots of onlookers. They drove around the block, up one street and down the next, through street-wide puddles where great wings of muddy water spewed out from under the wheels, drenching anyone who was slow in getting out of the way.

"Jeezus! Ain't that a sight! Ol' Moses is goin' to glory with a real splash, ain't he."

"For sure. It might be a little late, but that's what I call a real baptism. But lookit! They're gonna go through that big puddle alongside the Elks Hall. Those women will get soaked." Then Eddie saw Pa go out and wave the procession down. Pa went back to the Indian truck and spoke to the driver who had emerged from the cab and was trying to clear the windshield. Pa opened the hood and leaned over the fender, reaching down beside the motor.

"That's Charlie Dorset's old truck. Charlie never had nothing but trouble with it. It used to go through distributor caps like they was jellybeans. Every few hundred miles she'd just shut down with a crack in the distributor cap. There wasn't nothing you could do but put on a new one and away she'd go. Hunter got to keepin' a few on hand all the time just so Charlie could keep his truck on the go."

Several minutes went by. At last Pa closed the hood on the truck, the drivers resumed their places and the tow once more got under way. This time, the Indian truck started after being pulled only a few yards. The chain was detached and the truck, its passengers now bespattered and wet, wallowed its way out of town.

Eddie went over to join his father. "Is the coffin really in that truck?"

"Yes, it is. And now the truck and everyone in it is in a big dirty mess because of those two damn smart alecks." He reached in his pocket and pulled out a dollar. "Here, go down to the Chinaman's and buy some ice cream to take over to Auntie Barb's. I'll come up there in a little while. Your ma wants me to pick up a few groceries. But right now I'm goin' over to Hunter's Garage. Got something to say over there."

On the way home, Ruthie chattered about her visit with

Auntie Barb. She had marvelled at the sight of the ice cream which came in the same shape as a pound of butter and in three colours — white, pink and brown. Eddie himself wondered what could possibly be next. Pa seemed strangely quiet and gave only curt answers to any remarks directed his way. The afternoon had passed and Mamma would soon be putting supper on the table.

When they turned in to the yard, Eddie saw a democrat pulled up beside the barn. Visitors! He wondered who it might be. "Looks like Tony Howard's buggy," said Pa. "Your ma's been sorta expectin' them to come by." Eddie was pleased. The Howards had two sons, both near his age. They would be good company. "So let's unhitch the horses. You can take the groceries in while I look after Duke and Daisy."

Ruthie raced to the house, eager to tell Mamma about her visit with Auntie Barb. Eddie took his time. This time, it would be for him to break the news about Moses. And not just to kids, but to grown-ups too. He considered carefully what he might say. The Howard family knew Moses too. Just in the spring Moses had helped them with seeding. Eddie gathered the bags of groceries, turning over in his mind all that he had heard that afternoon. He headed for the house.

They were all in the kitchen, Mamma, Ruthie, Mr. and Mrs. Howard and both boys. They exchanged greetings. "So. Eddie, what's the news from town?"

Eddie swelled with importance. He paused. Everyone waited. "Old Moses. That old Moses Bearskin. He's a good Indian now."

Fun with
Dick and Jane

The snowstorm had ended sometime during the night and yesterday's sombre cloud cover had given way to a vast canopy of blue. The morning sun, still low in the sky, cast long shadows across the pristine blanket of snow that covered the partially treed landscape. It was bitterly cold, and except for the car, nothing was moving.

The car held two men. The driver, Greg Taylor, was a superintendent of schools for the Federal Department of Indian Affairs. A veteran of thirty years in the system, he was about to retire and was using his last few days of service to make one final circuit of his territory, savouring his good-byes and, at the same time, introducing his successor, Ross Watson, to whoever he thought might matter.

Taylor had to concentrate on his driving, for the new snow had covered the road and filled the ditches so evenly that he could not be sure of where the road surface actually lay. He could only steer a course approximately mid-way between the barbed wire fences or the thin walls of trees that lined both sides of the road allowance. "This new snow makes a pretty picture, but I'd gladly trade it for a clear track that I could follow."

"For sure," Watson agreed. "And the glare on the snow doesn't help either. I'm sitting here with my eyes half-shut."

"Yeah, I always try to have sunglasses with me. Especially in winter. They're part of my winter driving gear just like my parka and my mitts. Nobody should go out this time of year without survival equipment."

"I guess you're right. There are some long lonely roads out here."

"You better believe it. Cars these days are pretty reliable, but you shouldn't put too much confidence in them. They can still break down or get you stuck in a snowdrift."

"Or a mud hole. I wonder how these new ones with the automatic transmissions will work if you want to rock yourself out of a mud hole."

"I dunno. It'll be awhile before you find out. Don't expect his majesty's government to spend an extra buck just so you won't have to shift gears. Back before the war, we were lucky to get a car with a heater. On a cold day, I'd have to drive with a window partway down to keep the windshield from fogging over."

"Guess we've all gone through that. This car seems pretty comfortable."

"It's a '48 and not too bad. Except for trimming it's pretty well the same car as before the war — just like the '40s and the '41s. But I like it. It's the first new car I've had since 1940."

Taylor slowed as they approached a crossroad. In one corner of the intersection there was a squat ramshackle structure built mainly of logs, but with an elongated addition of sawn lumber stretching out from the rear. There was a hand-operated gasoline pump in front and several stacks of fence posts off to one side. White smoke curled from a metal chimney jutting out from the roof of the log portion. "A filling station out here?" queried Watson. "I'll bet he hasn't sold fifty gallons of gas since Christmas."

"Maybe not a lot of gasoline this time of year, but he'll have done a nice bit of business just the same. This place is much more than a filling station. It is the heart of the community out here. Morris Nussbaum was here well before most of the homesteaders. He started up as a trading post. Sold to the Indians whatever they needed: traps and guns and ammunition; knives and pots and pans; blankets; flour, tea and tobacco. In exchange, he took in furs and seneca root. Then, when the homesteaders started coming in, he'd organize crews of Indians to pick roots off the cleared fields or cut fence posts or do anything that needed to be done. He has quite a big stock of goods ... real good prices on fishing tackle, and a lot of loyal customers."

"Just Indians?"

"Not at all. All the local farmers buy from him. And a lot of people from town — even Prince Albert — come out here to buy stuff you can't find anywhere else. It makes a nice outing on a summer evening to put the kids in the car and drive out here to the Crossroads Store, even if it's only to buy some ice cream. There's a fair-sized lake in behind those trees with a nice beach and a picnic area. It's a pretty popular place all summer long, especially on Sundays. Morris and his wife are good sorts. They've worked hard all their lives and they've made a good living for themselves."

"Did they raise a family out here?"

"Sure did. Three boys and a girl. All spaced evenly apart — one every four years — and all of them educated and doing well."

"Are any of them still around here?"

"Good lord, no! While they were growing up, they all helped out in the store. They took their schooling by correspondence with the bigger kids helping the younger ones. Then they all helped put the oldest one through university. When he graduated and went to work, he helped out with the next one. They all made it. The youngest one is a doctor in Winnipeg. The girl is in Ottawa. If she were a man, she'd be a deputy minister by now. Another boy is an engineering professor in Saskatoon. The oldest is a chartered accountant. He was in the army during the war, a major in the Paymaster Corps. He married the only child of a man who owns a meat packing plant in Vancouver. That's where he is now, running the family business.

"It's an interesting place," Taylor continued. "On our way back, if it isn't too late, we'll drop in there and you can meet Morris and his missus. I took my son-in-law and grandson in there just before Christmas and we bought the kid a pair of Tackaberrys — as fine a pair of hockey skates as we could get anywhere. He's a big kid and one helluva hockey player — in his last year as a peewee. He'll be moving up to bantam next year and should have a good pair of skates."

"Kids grow so fast, he'll likely need a new pair next year."

"If he does, I'll see that he gets 'em. Scouts start noticing talent at the bantam age. If my grandson gets passed over, it won't be because he doesn't have a decent pair of skates."

"The owners here must be getting along in years."

"Oh yeah. The kids are all urging them to retire and move

to a city, but the old folks aren't in a hurry. They like what they're doing. They're a great couple and you'll enjoy knowing them. But, right now, we'd better keep on our way. Our priority is to visit Tall Pine School, where you will have the pleasure of meeting Miss Jane Schiller."

The school stood apart from an untidy scattering of decrepit cabins, some made from logs and others from rough-cut lumber. There didn't seem to be anyone out and about, for the new snow had not been disturbed. But for the smoke escaping from the stove-pipe chimneys, one could have thought the settlement to be deserted.

The L-shaped school building served a double purpose. The main part of the structure, the L's stem, was the classroom, while the L's foot provided living quarters for the teacher. Each section had an ample front step giving access to an entry door. The snow had not been swept from either set of steps and there were no footprints. Nosed in beside the steps to the teacherage was a blue sedan, its roof and hood bearing a thick mantle of snow. The two men ascended the school steps. Taylor showed his irritation. "Dammit! With these people, anything is a reason for staying away from school. After this snowstorm, I should have known that attendance would be zero. But let's have a look in. Miss Schiller will be glad to see us." He opened the door and they looked in. There was no one there.

"So-oo, let's check on the teacher." They descended the school steps and climbed the ones leading to the door of the teacherage. Taylor knocked. There was no response. They waited a moment and knocked again. There was still no answer. "Well, hell! What do you make of this? She can't have gone anywhere because her car is right there. It hasn't moved — at least not since yesterday. What do you think?"

"I think we'd better look in," Watson advised. "Maybe she needs help. She might be lying in there sick or in some kind of difficulty."

Taylor nodded. "You're right. Let's go in." He tried the door. It was locked. He knocked thunderously and tried the door again. "Anyone home?" he shouted. The house remained silent.

"Allow me," said Watson and he motioned Taylor aside. Then, placing himself at just the right distance, he raised one foot to doorknob height and, rocking forward, smashed the sole of his size twelve boot against the door. There was a heavy thump, the brief sound of splintering wood and the door burst inward.

The men found themselves confronted by a heavy set woman. Her short blonde hair was curly, but in disarray. She was wrapped in a light blue bathrobe belted around the middle with a braided rope of navy blue. Visible below her robe were broad bare feet and thick ankles. One hand was clutching the front of her robe and the other was raised to cover her mouth as if to suppress a scream.

Taylor spoke first. "Oh Miss Schiller! Thank God you're all right. We were worried about you. Sorry if we frightened you, but we felt that we had to come in."

Miss Schiller lowered her hand. "You didn't wait," she said accusingly.

"No, I'm afraid we didn't wait very long," Taylor conceded. "But we thought you might be caught in an emergency of some kind. Are you all right?"

"Yes, I'm ... no ... I've been sick. The flu. Since last week. Thursday."

"And how are you getting on? Have you seen a doctor? Do you have anyone to look after you? Is there anything that we can do for you?" Taylor was all solicitude.

"I ... I didn't know it was you. I thought it might have been ..." and her voice trailed off.

Watson spoke up. "If you have the flu, we'd better get you out of this cold doorway. Like it or not, we'll have to come in for a few minutes ... at least long enough to fix this door. We can't go away leaving it in this condition. We'll patch it up and you can go back to bed."

"Right," said Taylor, "this cold draft can't be doing you any good. We'll come in and size up the damage we did to your door. I have a tool kit in my car. A hammer and a few nails is all I'll need to make a temporary repair. Then I'll have one of the maintenance men come out to do the job right." He gestured toward Watson. "But I should introduce you to my associate. This is Ross Watson. He has just been appointed as superintendent and he'll be taking over from me in just a few days. And Ross. Meet Miss Jane Schiller. Miss Schiller came all the way from Ontario last August to take charge of Tall Pine Day School."

Miss Schiller didn't seem to notice the hand that Watson extended toward her. There was a growing awareness that she might have been wronged. This was a forced entry. An invasion. For no reason. Her face hardened and her pale eyes chilled. "You broke into my place ... my home. You had no right ..."

But Taylor broke in. "You are absolutely right. I see that now," he soothed. "But our intentions were good. For all we knew, you might have been lying there unconscious."

"Or worse," added Watson. "Maybe even dead."

"We really had no choice," Taylor placated. "Now I'll just fix this door as well as I can and we'll be on our way and out of your hair."

"You don't need to fix the door. I can do it," she began, but Taylor had already turned to go out to his car.

"We're really sorry about this," Watson apologized to the increasingly surly Miss Schiller.

She glared at him. "You don't need to stay. The door is okay. It can stay like that for a few days. Anyway, I can fix it." She turned her back.

Taylor was soon back with his tools and a short pole cut from a young poplar. One end of the pole forked to form a shallow Y. "Just prop this pole against the door with the fork under the knob. Then nobody can kick your door in the way Mr. Watson just did." Taylor was doing his best to allay the resentment he could read in Miss Schiller's sullen demeanour. He gathered up his tools and the few scattered splinters of wood. "Okay, I think this does it for now. So, Mr. Watson, we can now ask Miss Schiller's forgiveness, bid her farewell and get on our way. But I'll have to check the school register and sign it just to show that I was here, so we'll go out through the school." Two long strides brought him in front of the middle of three interior doors. He reached out to open it.

"No! Not that door," gasped Miss Schiller. "That's my pantry."

But Taylor had already pulled the door wide open. And there, slack-jawed and quaking with fear, stood an Indian boy. Stark naked. Skinny. Both hands down covering his genitals. There was a sharp intake of breath throughout the room and a long second of silence. Then the boy slid around Taylor and spurted toward the entry door.

"What the hell! Ross! Stop him! Catch that kid." But the boy eluded Watson's grasp and was out the door and down the steps in what seemed like one frantic leap.

The two men rushed to the door and saw the boy sprinting across the clearing toward the little cluster of cabins, seemingly unimpeded by the depth of the new snow. "Watch him, Ross. Watch where he goes. We'll have to get that kid. I need to talk to him. Don't let him get away," Taylor commanded. The boy disappeared into a cabin.

The two men turned to face Miss Schiller. Taylor swelled with suddenly assumed authority, all trace of affability gone. "Miss Schiller, go and get dressed. We have to talk." Then, turning to Watson, "Ross, would you find that kid and bring him back here? No, he's naked. We can't drag him out in the cold. Stay with him and talk to him right where you find him. Maybe his parents are there. Find out all you can."

Watson turned to go and then stopped. "The boy will want his clothes. "He won't talk to me if he's naked."

Taylor concurred. "You're right. Miss Schiller, fetch the boy's clothes and give them to Mr. Watson. Then we'll settle this matter. Right here and right now." He accompanied Watson to the door and faced him, grinning ruefully. "Sorry to involve you in this mess. It's my problem, but I hope you won't mind helping me out. I want to have this all settled and done with before we leave here today. I know what I'm going to do. We saw what we saw and there's only one explanation. But we'll need some sort of confirmation from the boy. Can you get it for me?"

Miss Schiller, now wearing slacks and a sweater, appeared and wordlessly handed Watson a small bundle of clothing.

"Is this all?" asked Watson. "No parka? No boots?"

"He wears moccasins," was her curt reply. "And his parka isn't here. Maybe it's in the school."

Following the boy's footprints, the bundle of clothing under his arm, Watson slogged through the snow to the cabin in which the boy had sought refuge. He knocked. The door opened immediately and he went inside.

Two hours later, Watson was back in the teacherage. Miss Schiller was nowhere to be seen. Taylor was seated at the kitchen table. He motioned to indicate that Miss Schiller was in the bedroom. "I believe we've settled things at this end. Miss Schiller has had an urgent call to return to Ontario and I have accepted her resignation as of the day before yesterday. So today she is not a teacher in the employ of the federal government nor is she a bona fide tenant of this residence which is reserved for the exclusive use of our teachers. She is a squatter with no right to be here. So whatever was going on here this morning was not between a student of ours and his teacher, but was between two trespassers.

"Miss Schiller tells me that she arrived here in August with only a couple of suitcases. It won't take her long to pack. That's what she's doing now. We will escort her to Prince Albert and that will bring this sorry business to an end."

"But the boy is a student," Watson pointed out. "At least that's what he told me."

"Not if I say he isn't," retorted Taylor. "He showed up here back in November and our Miss Schiller did not enter him properly in the school register. There is no record of his attendance here. He can become a student tomorrow if he likes, but today we don't know him. He is nothing to us. This business is over and done with." Taylor nodded emphatically and tilted backward in his chair.

"I see," mused Watson. "Over and done with is it? Would you like to hear what I found out? I've been busy too, you know."

"Of course. You went down there to get information and I want to hear it. What did you find out?"

"Well, his name is Richard Smoothstone — Dick to his friends — and he will be fifteen years old in April. He came here from Qu'Appelle last fall to stay with an aunt because his mother had taken off to Montana with a new man. Richard has been under Miss Schiller's ... ah ... protection since just before Christmas."

"How do you suppose that got started?"

"I suppose that she was just looking for someone and there he was. She fancied him and that was it. His auntie wasn't looking out for him very well. I think Miss Schiller has a kind of 'take charge' personality and the poor kid didn't have much of a chance. And besides, she did offer a powerful incentive."

"An incentive? You mean something other than the pleasure of Miss Schiller's loving embrace?"

"Now Greg, just listen and I will tell all. As I just told you, Dickie boy came from Qu'Appelle. He learned to play hockey down there. He loves the game and, from what these people told me, is very good at it — certainly far better than any of the kids he played with on the reserve. Someone noticed him and last year he was invited to play with the bantam team in town. Apparently the team went all the way to the provincial finals and he was their top scorer."

"And then?"

"And then he had to come up here, bringing only the clothes on his back. He had no hockey equipment, not even skates."

"Oh yeah. And they play hockey here out on the lake.

They put up a board fence as soon as the ice is thick enough."

"Exactly. And there he is, the best young hockey player in the whole northeast having to get along with whatever cast-off equipment he can scrounge."

"I'm beginning to see. Is this where Miss Schiller comes to the rescue?"

"Right on! Miss Schiller promised to supply everything for a complete hockey outfit right from the jockstrap out. Stuff the kid had only dreamt of owning. And he's a Chicago Blackhawks fan. You know — Max and Doug Bentley — so along with everything else, the kid wanted a Blackhawk jersey."

"I can understand that. Did she come across?"

"Not as readily as he did."

"Just what do you mean by that?"

"Well, he gave his all at their first private session, but he didn't get the whole package all at once. He had to earn it a bit at a time. First the shin pads, then the shoulder pads, then the gloves and so on. He has everything now except the skates and a new stick. The first stick got broken. He might have got the skates tonight if we hadn't happened to turn up."

"Christalmighty! What a situation! So the skates are here?"

"So he says. She has them. He's seen them. Tackaberrys. Apparently your Crossroads merchant has sold two or three pair out here this winter. They're viewed as reverently as the bones of a saint."

"Well that kid has certainly earned them. Poor little fart."

"Don't feel too sorry for him. Apparently he's done his bit of swaggering around, enjoying his role as the teacher's stud."

"Of course none of this is a secret."

"Hardly."

Taylor sat thoughtfully stroking his chin. Then he turned toward the bedroom and shouted, "Miss Schiller, can you hear me?" Miss Schiller could. She appeared in the doorway, now dressed for travel. "Miss Schiller, have you packed those Tackaberry skates?" Miss Schiller turned back into the bedroom only to emerge a moment later with the skates still in their carton and an immaculate hockey stick. She dropped them on the floor and silently returned to the bedroom.

Taylor addressed himself again to the bedroom door. "Miss Schiller, I see your car keys right here on the kitchen counter. Mr. Watson and I will start your car and warm it up for you. If it needs a boost, I have booster cables with me. We will follow you to Prince Albert. If we are to get there before dark, we should start out within the next half-hour. But first, Mr. Watson and I are going to deliver the Tackaberry skates and the stick to Richard." Then he turned to Watson. "I still think the kid has them coming."

Something over a year went by. Taylor and Watson met by chance in a Vancouver shopping mall, their first encounter since their visit to Tall Pine Day School. They went for coffee.

Watson seemed to have a private joke. He said, "I'm sure you remember our visit to Tall Pine School that cold winter day a year ago."

"How could I forget?"

"And the delectable Miss Schiller?"

"Equally unforgettable."

"Well, she's back with us."

Taylor couldn't conceal his astonishment. "Back? At Tall Pine? Surely not! She wouldn't dare. Not teaching I hope."

"No, she's given up teaching. She's her own boss and

nobody can fire her now. You see, she's the new owner of the Crossroads Store. And young Dick is the captain of the Tall Pine Blackhawks, the best dressed hockey team in the entire northeast."

That's Just
the Way It Was

You got all them empty tables to choose from mister, but you might just as well set down right here with me. Then we'll both have somebody to talk to. I bin sittin' here by myself for too damn long ... just sittin' here and watchin' them Hutterite boys tear down that store building across the street.

So what'll you have? A Bo? Hey Myrtle, bring us a couple Bohemians ... and bring this gent a glass. No ... no. Thisuns on me.

Time was on a Sattiday, this place'd be a-hoppin'. You couldn't find a place to sit, an' now lookit ... 'cept for me an' you an' them two fellas over in the corner the place is empty. Two ... mebbe three owners retired rich from this hotel. Bill Gransby who built 'er an' Pat O'Hara who took 'er over from Bill. They done real good, but she's changed hands over an' over since then, an' the poor stiff what's got 'er now can't hardly pay hisself wages. I bet he wishes he'd never heard of Hastings.

Yep, I was born right here in Hastings an' lived 'round here for most o'my life 'cept for when I was overseas in the war. Mebbe I shouldn't of come back here, but how was anyone to know that Hastings would come down to nothin'? This useta be a busy town ... divis'nal point for the CNR ... we had ever'thing ... the roundhouse ... coal dock ... water tank ... an' about nine men workin' in the station. Now there ain't none of it left ... even the station is gone. The whole town ... it's all of it gone ... the grain elevators ... the hospital ... the drugstore ... the car and implement dealers ... the poolroom an' the bakery ... just empty run-down buildings is all that's left.

An' now them Hutterite boys is tearin' down the store where I started work. That was way back before the war when I was just a kid. Benson's Department Store ... the best an' busiest store between Saskatoon an' Winnipeg ... groceries ... hardware ... clothes ... furnicher ... vetin'rary supplies ... you name it. If they was anything you needed, you could get it at Benson's. If Tom Benson didn't have it in stock, he'd have it down on the nex' train, an' we had two trains a day in them days. Open at nine ever' mornin' 'cept Sunday an' didn't close on Sattiday night till the last customer was gone ... mebbe not till midnight. That's just the way it was. Ever'body thought it was all gonna last forever. An' now, that store buildin' is gonna be a pigpen or a calvin' shed out on the Hutterite colony.

After the war, Tom Benson wanted me to come back an' work in the store. In a way, I would of liked to, but I had got married just before I went overseas an' my wife's folks had this nice farm northa town. They had only the one kid ... my wife ... an' they wanted us to help out on the farm for a few years an' then take it over. I had some vet'ran's credits from my time in the army so I bought me a half section just down the road from the old folks an' that's purty well bin the story of my life up to now. It's turned out good enough, but I sure liked workin' in that store.

I still helped out there some whenever they was a little slack time on the farm. Tom Benson had quite a few workin' for him an' some was good an' some wasn't so hot, but if I had a little time, he'd allus have somethin' for me to do ... mostly in the hardware or makin' heavy deliveries.

While I was in the army, Tom hired this young fella from over towards Red Rock Valley. He was a real smart fella ... would of joined up, but couldn't pass the medical ... polio when he was a kid left him with a bad leg. Not real bad, but he'd limp a little by the end o' the day an' he didn't go in for no sports or dancing. But he sure learned the store business in a hurry. It was as if that store was where he was meant to be. Just a year or so an' he was like Tom's right arm. He knew ever'thing they had to do in that store. He could set up a furnace or cut up a half of beef an' he could fix anything that needed fixin'. An' he helped Tom with the books too. Lots o' times when the trav'lers came out from the wholesalers, Tom would have them talk to Willie an' Willie would do the orderin'. That was his name, Willie ... Willie Boronski. We worked together quite a bit whenever I was in the store an' we got to be purty good friends.

Tom had two boys ... they was both a fair bit younger 'en me. Even as kids they helped out in the store ... Tom saw to that. They started out deliverin' groceries an' doin' chores aroun' the place. The oldest kid, Tommy, was a bookish sort who didn't take much to mixin' with folks ... he did what his dad told him to do an' he was polite to the customers, but I could see that he wasn't goin' to be no helluva store-keeper, an' I think Tom saw it too. Anyways, Tommy joined the air force right outa high school an' after the war he never came back here to Hastings, 'cept mebbe for visits. He went to university for more years than I can count an' now he's a perfesser in Montreal ... dunno why he went there ... nothing there but Frenchies ... but I guess you go to where the job is. The job don't often come lookin' for you no matter how much eddication you got.

Lookit. They got the roof boards stripped off. Won't take 'em long now to knock down the rafters ... them Hutterite boys know how to work ... they can sure hustle ... special if some high school girls happen to walk by.

There's some folks here what blames the Hutterites for the town goin' back the way it has, but I don't see it that way. It ain't the Hutterites what made the CN switch over to die-sels an' shut down the branch lines an' it ain't the Hutterites what's buyin' up all the land. Sure, so they bought up some, but I got a neighbour what's got more land than the whole colony. An' that's just one man an' there's others like 'im.

The kid brother? That was Rocky. His real name was Wendel ... that was his ma's maiden name. She was from Saskatoon an' her old man was Wendel Insurance. He was in real estate too an' was pretty well fixed. Anyways, when Rocky was just a little tad, folks got to callin' him Wendy. That was okay till he started school an' found out there was some girls named Wendy. From then on, his name had to be Rocky. He wasn't gonna answer to no girl's name. If some'n tried callin' him Wendy, the fight was on. With a bunch o' scrappy kids there was quite a few bloody noses an' tore up shirts before ever'body unnerstood that his name was Rocky an' that anyone who wanted to call him Wendy had better have his fists up.

He wasn't no bookworm like Tommy. He was all hot to get into the air force too, but by the time he finished high school, the war was windin' down an' the air force didn't need no more men ... too bad he couldn't of joined up. Some o' that military discipline might of done 'im some good. Anyways, he went to work in the store an' I s'pose he expected to take it over whenever Tom decided to call it quits.

In some ways he was good in the store ... real good ... had a nice way with customers ... remembered their names even if they was from forty miles away an' came inta the store only two or three times a year ... could talk easy about nothin' ... could seem to be just as interested in the price o' oats as in las' night's hockey game. But when it came time to get down to business an' gettin' the customer what he wanted ... like mebbe a hunnert pound sack o' flour ... Rocky would turn 'im over to one o' the other clerks to do the fetchin' an' carryin'. I seen it an' he done it to me often enough. Then he'd go over an' hold out the glad hand to another customer. He was all pers'nality an' no sweat, but he got away with it. Yeah. Boss's son. That's just the way it was.

Well, yeah. Another Bo sounds good. I still got the thirst an' I still got the time. The wife's over 'cross town at some kinda hen party ... when she's finished, she knows where to find me. A cold beer runs down purty easy don't it?

Times was good in them days right after the war. Ever'body ... even us farmers ... had a little extra cash an' some o' the business men in town was doin' real good. They was makin' so much money that they just had to find ways to get rid of it. So it was only nat'ral that they should get to pla-yin' poker ... in their homes at first, but when it started gettin' serious an' the stakes was gettin' high, they come down to play here in the hotel. Pat O'Hara ... he had the hotel then ... Pat set up a room just for poker. But he didn't take no rake-off nor nothin'. He was a pretty sharp kinda card player hisself an' he likely won more'n his share o' the pots.

Stakes got purty high sometimes an' a lot o' money ... thousands o' dollars could cross the table in one night. The reg'lar players took to callin' theirselves "The Board" an' their poker sessions was Board meetin's. In a way, they sorta ran the town ... some o' them was town councillors an' just as much o' the town's business got talked over and settled at those poker sessions as at council meetin's.

Did I play? Nosir. Not me. I didn't have pockets deep enough to mix with that crew. I allus worked hard for my money an' I ain't gonna lose it in no card game ... an' I wouldn't wanta take no money offa somebody else neither. Anyways, my wallet wasn't fat enough to get me an invite to join the Board.

Tom Benson was a reg'lar player an' one o' the lucky ones. One time he won a quarter section o' land ... then he rented it right back to the fella who lost it ... a farmer from down there west o' Stockdale ... an' Tom collected a third o' the crop from that quarter until the farmer was able to buy it back. They say the guy's wife never did find out that he had lost that quarter. It don't make no kind o' sense to me, but that's just the way it was.

All this time Willie was pluggin' away in the store here ... workin' hard an' not makin' no fuss. Most people took him for grannet an' couldn't bother to see that he was really runnin' the whole kaboodle. Tom was away to the city quite a bit an' he was tied up with a dozen differ'nt clubs an' org'nizations. So Willie was the real manager, but nobody ever thought o' him that way. He done the work, but he didn't have the name or the pay.

It seems he didn't expeck much for hisself ... he wasn't married ... never had a girlfriend ... mebbe he thought because of his bad leg that girls wouldn't be int'rested ... I dunno ... Anyways he lived real quiet in a little house he rented from Tom Benson ... bought a second-hand half-ton that he'd drive out to see his folks on a Sunday or sometimes out to my place for supper. You'd of thought he had all he wanted in life in that store even though nothin' in it was his an' never would be. I useta wonder how things would turn out after Tom quit an' turned things over to Rocky.

That day came sooner than anyone expected. Early one mornin' ... before breakfas' it was ... I get a call from Willie. He asked if I could go with him to Saskatoon. They had got word that Tom had dropped dead in there ... heart attack or somethin' they thought. Rocky was out at the coast on his honeymoon an' Missus Benson asked Willie to go in to Saskatoon an' make arrangements to have Tom's body brought back to Hastings. Willie wanted me along so's I could drive Tom's car back.

Tom's dyin' so sudden like that was a shock to ever'body, but that was only the half of it. Tom's body was still at the hospital. We identified it an' all that an' was about to go see an undertaker when Willie remembered to ask about Tom's clothes an' stuff. But they told us there wasn't none. They said an amb'lance had brought Tom in on a stretcher with only a blanket over 'im an' there wasn't no clothes. We knew Tom allus stayed at the Bessborough so we went there. When we told the manager what had happened, he took us up to Tom's room, but there wasn't nothin' there either ... just Tom's suitcase an' half a bottle of rye. The manager told us that there hadn't bin no amb'lance at the hotel for over a month an' that Tom must of bin picked up somewheres else. So Willie called up the amb'lance people to find out where they had picked Tom up from. They gave us the address, but the guy said that he thought he better warn us that the place was a hoor house ... but o' course we still had to go there. Willie didn't have no comment about Tom conkin' out in a hoor house ... all he said was it was lucky Missus Benson hadn't come along.

We found the place all right even though it didn't have no big electric sign up on the roof. Tom's Buick was right there on the street. The woman inside was expectin' somebody to come. She had Tom's clothes folded up real neat with his hat on top o' the pile. Then she handed over the car keys and the wallet. Willie took the wallet an' started to look inside, but the woman said that Tom's money was all there an' that they wasn't thieves in that place. They was just hoors. Then she said that Tom was a nice man an' she was sorry he died. When we left, she said we should come back again.

Humpin' that hoor was one helluva way for Tom to conk out, but the send-off Hastings gave him was something else. It was the biggest funeral I ever seen ... the church was overflowin' an' the p'rade out to the cemetery was near a mile long. Willie an' me didn't tell nobody where Tom had took his heart attack. It was nobody's business an' both of us had allus got along good with Tom. Like the hoor said, Tom was a nice man.

So anyways, Rocky figgered he'd be fillin' his dad's boots

... an' not just Rocky ... purty near ever'body else did too. Only a few of us saw that Rocky was all flash an' no bang an' that it would be up to Willie to make that store hang together. An' that's just the way it was.

Rocky would roll inta the store mebbe around nine-thirty ... just in time to go out for coffee. Then he'd come back in an hour or so just to amble in an' out an' give orders an' talk big deals.

An' Willie was workin' twice as hard as before. He tol' me he had to set Rocky straight a couple o' times 'cause he was helpin' hisself to a few big bills right outa the cash drawer. Willie tol' him to go ahead an' pay hisself whatever wages he wanted, but to quit raidin' the till. There was no way Willie could keep a good set o' books if the boss wasn't playin' straight.

An' that's just the way it was for the next year or two. The two o' them seemed to get along okay ... at least as far as most people could tell. Willie cared too much about that store an' the Benson name to right out have a quar'l with his new boss an' Rocky was just smart enough to see how much he needed Willie.

What happened next I wouldn't have believed it in a million years 'cept I know it's true. There was a fella in town ... name of Gord Kimball ... had played perfessional hockey ... was up there with the Leafs for a few years ... you might of heard of 'im but this was a long time ago ... way back before your time. Anyways, he got hisself set up in the machinery business ... had the John Deere in Hastings ... an' that for sure was one helluva dealership. He had a half dozen salesmen out on the road all the time ... fannin' out all over hell's half acre an' he was puttin' out carloads of machinery. He was a mean cuss an' he was rough on ever'body ... wouldn't give nobody a break ... not like Tom Benson.

They say he was hard on his wife too ... she was from down east ... Tronna mebbe ... an' they got hitched while he was still playin' hockey. Quite a looker she was, but she would of bin even better if she didn't have to live with Kimball. Like I said, he was a mean cuss ... hard on ever'body.

I dunno how Willie an' her ever got mixed up together. Likely Willie had to go over to fix their furnace or somethin' an' then fate took over an' tumbled 'em both inta bed. Was prob'ly the first time Willie ever got laid ... an' when he found out what it was like, he was just a-snortin' for more.

But the trouble with a place like Hastings is that it ain't big enough. Ever'body knows who you are an' where ya bin an' where ya goin'. There wasn't no place in town where they could meet an' Willie couldn't keep makin' service calls for-ever to Kimball's house. What they hit on was to meet on Sunday afternoons out on some pasture land not far from where Willie's folks lived. It was along the river hills where there was clumps of trees an' lots of places that was nice and private.

That was fine till berry pickin' time. Then one nice sunny afternoon, Willie an' his lady friend ... she must of bin forty-five or thereabout ... a good fifteen years older 'n Willie ... they was out in their special spot carryin' on as usual. The thing is that they didn't know that Jessie Hyde was already out scoutin' for saskatoon berries. She had walked in from a differ'nt road an' was just amblin' along when she come around a bush an' there they was. If it had of bin me, I'd of backed off an' left 'em go to it. But not Jessie ... Jessie was a screamer ... if a flea farted, Jessie'd scream ... so o'course this time she let out with a humdinger that would of stopped a war.

Jessie didn't announce it at church or nothin', but mebbe

she tol' her best friend. Hastings hadn't had a piece o' gossip like that in a long time, an' before the week was half over ever'body had tol' ever'body else at leas' three times. I dunno how Kimball an' his wife settled things ... but Kimball hisself had a purty spotty record ... he couldn't throw nothin' at her that she couldn't throw right back at him. I guess they managed to work somethin' out.

But it was differ'nt with Willie. The poker playin' crowd was all in Kimball's corner. Kimball was one o' them ... a member of The Board. An' they couldn't let no gimpy legged little bohunk from Red Rock Valley get away with bangin' the wife o' no Board member. Willie would have to go.

It was settled at a Board meetin' ... Kimball wasn't there but most o' the others includin' Rocky was. Rocky didn't have the guts to face up to the others. He let 'em tell him what to do, even if it meant big trouble for Benson's Department Store. The whole gang went over to Willie's place an' roused him outa bed. They gave him twenny-four hours to get outa town or risk bein' gelded. Willie was gone before daylight.

It was like from that day the town started goin' downhill. First it was the store. Rocky couldn't run it without Willie. He still had to play the big shot with cigars an' booze an' long holiday trips ev'ry summer ... an' that wife o' his was just as good at spendin' money as Rocky hisself ... o' course he had to keep on playin' poker an' he wasn't none too good at that neither.

You wouldn't believe that a good business like that could be run inta the ground so fast, but Rocky managed it in less 'n two years. The clerks was quittin' 'cause they wasn't gettin' paid ... the wholesalers cut 'im off an' the bank wouldn't bail 'im out. He hadta close the doors. That's just the way it was.

Then it was the railroad cuttin' back an' the gover'ment buildin' a new highway to Saskatoon. You wanna kill a town like Hastings, all you gotta do is build a highway to the city. Mebbe folks get bargains in the city, but now they can drive a hunnert miles for a loaf o' bread. The car dealers all went ... an' the hospital an' the drugstore an' the bank. All we got left is the school an' the credit union. There ain't enough curlers left even to pay the light bill in the rink ... I s'pose it'll be the nex' buidin' to be tore down.

Hey Myrt! Let's have a couple more here. We still got a long day ahead of us.

Willie? Oh, Willie's okay. He landed on his feet. All the wholesalers knew him for a good man an' right away they was steerin' job offers his way. He wasn't outa work hardly at all. He's done real good for hisself. Gettin' fired an' run outa town was the best thing ... nex' to gettin' laid ... that ever happened to Willie. He's out at the coast now ... married with growed-up kids ... has a Handy Hardware franchise for three stores out there. He's a millionaire over an' over again. An' to think that he had his start in that wreck of a buildin' across the street. But that's just the way it was.

TGIF

Kirsten liked school so much that she hardly ever looked forward to the weekend, but this Friday was so special that she had not been able to contain her eagerness. It would be the start of a wonderful weekend. There were so many good things going to happen.

She woke to the realization that this was the day. Friday. T G I F. On a Friday, the big kids in school would sometimes sigh and roll their eyes and say, "T G I F," pretending that they could hardly wait to escape, but Kirsten knew that they didn't really mean it. But today, the words just popped into her head, "Thank God it's Friday," and she meant them.

From her bed, she could see blue sky through the window, so knew it would be a sunny day. Mama was busy downstairs. Kirsten could hear the table being set for breakfast and could smell the coffee. The screen door slammed. That would be Ivar coming in from harnessing Thor.

Kirsten allowed herself a small grimace. Thor was the only problem. It would be embarrassing if he farted while they were bringing Miss Stanton home. And he did fart so much. So much so that Papa had named him "Thor" after the god of thunder. The very day that Papa and Ivar had brought him home from Grimstad's auction sale and Papa called for her to come out to see their new buggy horse, Thor had shown what he could do. They were all there, the whole family, Mama and Elsa and the baby and even Knut, the hired man. Then Thor rumbled away, on and on and on, just as if he would never stop. Everyone was startled into silence until Knut looked up at the sky and then around at the family and said, "Dat's fonny. T'onder but no lightning?"

Everyone laughed. Especially Ivar. Ivar thought it was so funny. Now, every time Thor let one go, Ivar would imitate Knut and say, "T'onder but no lightning?" All the boys in school had taken up the joke. One of them would make a farting noise and then they would all look out the window, pretending to be puzzled.

Miss Stanton was from the city and didn't understand, but she'd be cross if she ever caught on. Kirsten was mad at Ivar. He thought he was so smart because he was eleven and she was only eight. But today, for once, maybe Thor would behave himself.

She heard the door slam again and the sound of men's voices. Papa and Knut had come in for breakfast. She had better hurry. The men would be washing up in the back porch. She would have to wait to wash until after breakfast. Then mama would comb and braid her hair and put up the braids in the Norwegian way. Kirsten wanted to look nice for Miss Stanton. Miss Stanton was so pretty and wore such stylish clothes. Kirsten wished that Mama had dresses like Miss Stanton's. Of course they wouldn't do for everyday around the farm, but maybe for best, for church or for visiting.

Kirsten sighed happily. Today was going to be perfect. Miss Stanton was going to come and stay with them for the whole weekend. After school, she would come home in the buggy with Ivar and her and would stay overnight. On Saturday, there would be so many things to show. The secret place in the trees where she had made her playhouse and the new kittens in the hayloft. The baby pigs were so cute when they were little. It was too bad that they had grown so big so quickly. But she could still show Miss Stanton the snapshot of her holding a tiny pig wrapped in a towel, just like a baby.

Then on Saturday after supper Papa would take them all to town in the car. That would be wonderful. The car was new and shiny. They had used it only a few times, only to church and over to Oncle Sverre's. It was a touring car. Maybe Papa would fold the top down and everyone would see that Miss Stanton was with them and would know that she was staying with them for overnight. On Sunday, Mama would make a special breakfast and they would all go to church. And after church there would be a chicken dinner with maybe other company coming. They never knew who might come for dinner on a Sunday. There always seemed to be someone who would come to their place after church. She hoped Oncle Sverre would come so her cousins could see what a nice teacher she had. Her cousins went to a different school and had a man for a teacher. Just an ordinary man.

Breakfast over, she was washed and ready for school. Mama had let her wear her blue dress with the white collar. It used to be her best dress, but would soon be too small.

Mama said she should get a little more wear out of it while she could. She was growing so fast.

Ivar had hitched Thor to the buggy and was waiting for her. Kirsten picked up the two lunch pails. Hers had a picture of a squirrel with a big bushy tail curled over its back. Mama had bought it filled with peanut butter. Ivar's was red with a big green leaf on it. "A shamrock," Mama had said. The lettering on it spelled PURE LARD.

Ivar was wearing his new winter coat with the fur collar. Kirsten smiled to herself. The weather wasn't cold enough yet for a winter coat. She knew that Ivar too wanted to dress up for Miss Stanton. She would tease him later. If she said anything now, he might go in and change to his old coat. Just to be mean. She'd wait until they were far enough along the way that he couldn't turn back. Then she'd tease him about liking Miss Stanton.

Kirsten tucked the lunch pails in with the oatsheaf behind the seat and clambered in to sit beside Ivar. Of course Thor had to start out farting at every step and Ivar had to say, "T'onder but no lightning?" It wasn't funny. If they did that on the way home with Miss Stanton along, she would just die from embarrassment. Her lower lip trembled as she considered the awful possibility.

Half a mile along their way, they were joined by another rig which had pulled out from a lane to follow close behind them. It was the Sandviks. There were five of them. The three biggest sat crowded on the seat while Erik and Olaf, the twins, who were only seven, stood behind.

They all called back and forth to each other and Leif Sandvik, who was in Grade Eight, tried to tease them about their horse. "Cover your ears," he advised everyone. "Thor the Thunder Maker might decide to let one go and deafen us all."

But Ivar was clever and wouldn't be teased. "It ain't always thunder," he boasted. "Last night he played 'Turkey in the Straw.' Once he's learned a few more tunes, Papa's going to hire him out for barn dances." Kirsten giggled in spite of herself. Sometimes she was proud of Ivar. He always had an answer for the bigger boys.

≈

In the schoolyard, Kirsten dismounted from the buggy and went to put her lunch pail in the cloakroom. On the way she was joined by Aldis Vestman and Ingrid Dalsrud who were also in Grade Three. They were best friends. They went in to see Miss Stanton. She was at her desk surrounded by a cluster of bigger girls. Kirsten stood quietly, hoping that Miss Stanton would notice her. Miss Stanton saw her and smiled. It was a beautiful smile. Miss Stanton's teeth were so white and so even. "A big welcome for Grade Three," she said. "But don't take your coats off. There's still a few minutes before bell time. Let's all go out and enjoy the outdoors until we have to get to work. The mornings are frosty now and it will soon be too cold to be outside." Rising, she led the girls out into the schoolyard. She had taken Aldis by one hand and Kirsten by the other. Kirsten smiled. The school day was beginning exactly as it should.

The schoolroom was crowded with eight grades. Miss Stanton took attendance. "Everyone is here today," she announced. "All thirty-nine of us or all forty, if you count me. It's been a good week for attendance. The rainy beginning has kept you big boys out of the harvest fields and in school. It's so nice to have you here." She smiled at the boys. They shuffled self-consciously. Some of the boys were big, maybe fifteen or sixteen. But Miss Stanton was older. The bigger girls guessed that she was twenty or maybe even twenty-one.

Kirsten was good at schoolwork. She noted with satisfaction the additions to the gold stars in her spelling and arithmetic scribblers. She had more gold stars than either Aldis or Ingrid. And although she was only in Grade Three, her handwriting was already better than Ivar's. And Ivar was in Grade Six. She worked carefully, allowing only a few whispered interruptions from her friends. She didn't want to be scolded. Especially not today. Today had to be perfect.

Morning recess was over. They had played tag and prisoners' base. But it was over too soon. Maybe, because it was a Friday, Miss Stanton would give them a longer afternoon recess.

Miss Stanton was teaching geography to Grade Eight. It was about Japan. Kirsten had finished her work and was listening to the geography lesson. "Victoria, I think you are ten thousand miles away. You haven't heard a word I've said for at least the last ten minutes." Miss Stanton was speaking to Victoria Wilkins.

"Maybe she's in Japan," said Leif and everyone tittered. Kirsten had noticed that Victoria was not her usual self. Her eyes were puffy and red as if she had been crying. And she hadn't joined in any games at recess, but had stayed alone, lingering near the school door. Kirsten looked across the room at Victoria, studying her thoughtfully. Victoria put on a show of activity, sitting up straight and shuffling books and papers and speaking up brightly to answer questions. But that behaviour didn't last long. Victoria was soon as far away as ever. Kirsten wondered what Victoria was thinking about. What could be more important than listening to Miss Stanton?

At noon the children, lunch pails in hand, scattered. Most of the smaller girls sat at their desks while they ate their lunch, but the bigger ones went outside. Ivar and some of the other boys had to go to the barn to feed their horses. Kirsten knew that sometimes the boys would climb up onto the barn roof on the side away from the school where Miss Stanton wouldn't see them. When they came down, they would smell of tobacco smoke. Kirsten hoped that Miss Stanton would catch them someday. But not today. It wouldn't do for Ivar to get into trouble today. Today had to be perfect.

The Grade Seven and Eight girls were sitting on the school steps where it was sunny and warm. The Grade Threes were close by and Kirsten could hear Victoria Wilkins above all the others. She was talking more than anyone else and was laughing at everything that anyone said. Even her laughter was different. So loud and shrill.

"I have some very special sandwiches that I made myself. Egg salad. Would anyone like to try one?" Victoria held out a sandwich toward the other girls. "No, I think I better keep them for myself. I might need them all." She withdrew her hand and raised the sandwich to her mouth, but she didn't bite into it. "I think I'll go in and get some water." She rose and went into the cloakroom where the water bucket was kept. The other girls exchanged puzzled looks and shifted about uneasily. Kirsten and her friends finished their lunch and went off to play.

First thing in the afternoon was story time, the part of the day that Kirsten enjoyed most. Miss Stanton would read a chapter from *The Adventures of Tom Sawyer*. Kirsten thought it a wonderful story. This day's chapter was the one where Tom tries to give his tonic to the cat. Kirsten couldn't help but laugh out loud even if it was too bad that Tom was mean to the cat. The description was so funny. Even Miss Stanton was laughing so hard that she had to stop reading for a little while.

After the story, the children got busy at their work. Kirsten hoped that everyone would behave so that Miss Stanton would let them have a spelling bee after recess. Kirsten was a good speller and could spell down kids in Grade Four or Five, especially boys. She liked to be on a team with Victoria because Victoria was the best speller in school. Kirsten noticed that Victoria's desk was empty. She was nowhere in the room. Where was she? Kirsten hadn't seen her leave.

Time passed. Kirsten had finished her work and was free to read a storybook. The room was quiet except for some restlessness among the big girls. Sigrid Felstad asked permission to leave the room. Miss Stanton looked around and noticed that Victoria was missing. "Wait till Victoria comes back," she said. "Then you can go."

"But Victoria's been gone such a long time," objected Sigrid. "She went out while you were reading the story."

"Very well. Just remember we'll take up Grade Eight science before recess and I want both of you back in here in less than no time." Miss Stanton pretended to be severe.

It seemed to be less than no time when the door burst open and a frightened Sigrid appeared, gasping and crying. "Oh Miss Stanton! Come! It's Victoria. She's in the girls' toilet. I think she's awful sick."

Miss Stanton dropped the book she was holding, commanded everyone to stay seated and ran outside. Some of the older pupils rushed to the windows. Kirsten's desk was in the row next to the windows. She couldn't stop herself from standing up. She saw Miss Stanton, with skirt raised almost knee high, racing along the pathway to the girls' toilet. Sigrid was with her. When they got there, they seemed to have some difficulty with the door. It was supposed to open inward, but something was blocking it. Miss Stanton and Sigrid struggled briefly with the door and then Sigrid came running back to the school.

"We need help! Miss Stanton wants the Grade Eights. Just the Grade Eights!" she cried, then turned and ran back with the four other Grade Eight pupils in close pursuit.

Kirsten saw the boys pushing on the door until they got it open far enough for Miss Stanton to squeeze through. A moment later, Bjorn Selbo also squeezed in. Then the door opened wider and Miss Stanton and Bjorn appeared half carrying and half dragging Victoria toward the school. After a few steps, Leif took Miss Stanton's place and the two boys, with Victoria between them, struggled further toward the school. Miss Stanton hurried ahead.

"Victoria is terribly sick. Who can go for her parents?"

Einar Olson spoke up. "I'll go. I ride horseback. That's the fastest."

"Then go. Tell them to come right away. I don't know what's wrong, but Victoria is terribly sick and I don't know what to do. Tell them to hurry. Oh, if only we had a telephone!"

Kirsten nodded. Telephones are important. Papa had helped to form a telephone company. Poles had been set along the roadsides and across some fields, and rolls of wire were there, waiting to be strung. Some families already had telephones mounted on their living room walls, but nobody had a telephone that worked.

"Ivar, could your father come with the car? Could you and Kirsten go home and have him come with the car?"

"Papa won't be at home. He was going to go into town for a telephone meeting. And Knut is taking the threshing outfit over to Oncle Sverre's. Mama is home alone with Elsa and the baby."

The boys brought Victoria into the schoolroom and tried to take her to her desk, but she couldn't sit up. She was moaning and her arms and legs were twitching. She seemed to have no control over them.

"We'll have to let her lie down. Bring her over here by my desk," ordered Miss Stanton. The boys did as they were told. Miss Stanton helped lay Victoria on the floor. Victoria kept struggling, arching her back and thumping the floor with her head. Miss Stanton went to the cloakroom and brought back two coats, her own and Ivar's. She folded Ivar's to make a pillow and used hers to cover Victoria.

"We can't have any more school today. I'll have to look after Victoria. You are all dismissed. I want you to go home and look for help. Tell your parents what has happened and have them come or send any help they can. But not the Grade Eight girls. I want you to stay here until more help comes."

"I could go down to the crossroads," offered Ivar. "It isn't far. Maybe someone will come driving along and I could stop them."

"Oh yes, Ivar. Do that. And please hurry." Children were leaving the schoolroom and hurriedly making their way across the yard toward the barn to get their horses. Soon, most of the children except for those who had to wait for their older sisters in Grade Eight were gone.

Kirsten, not wanting to be in the way, remained at her desk. Maybe Victoria would get better as quickly as she had got sick and Miss Stanton could still come for the weekend. She opened her storybook and tried to concentrate on the printed words.

Miss Stanton, on her knees, was trying to talk to Victoria. "What is it, Victoria? Can you tell me what is the matter? I don't know what's happening to you."

Victoria moaned something in reply.

Miss Stanton looked up at the Grade Eights who were grouped around her. "Poison! Oh dear! She's taken poison. What could it be? Where could she get it?" She turned to Victoria and questioned her again.

Again, Victoria's reply was barely audible. Kirsten couldn't hear what she had said.

"Gopher poison! In her sandwiches!" Miss Stanton reported to the Grade Eights. "Do any of you know anything about gopher poison?"

"Just that it works," said Leif.

"But what's in it? Is it arsenic or ... or what? Is there an antidote? Is there anything we can give her?"

No one knew of anything that might help.

Victoria continued to writhe beneath Miss Stanton's coat and drummed the floor with heels and fists.

"Maybe some water. Water might weaken the poison," someone suggested. Water was brought in the tin drinking cup. Miss Stanton raised Victoria to a near-sitting position and held the cup to her lips. Victoria made a horrible gagging noise and water came spewing out of her mouth.

"She doesn't seem able to swallow," said Miss Stanton. Her sleeve was all wet. "Should we try again, Victoria?

Would you like some water?" Victoria didn't answer. Miss Stanton laid her down again.

Kirsten shivered. She decided to go outside. Eric and Olaf were out there and Olise Nordbro. They'd be scared too. They could all wait together. As she stood up, she looked out the window. There was Einar on his horse coming at full gallop. "Miss Stanton! Here's Einar come back!" she exclaimed. A moment later, Einar was in the room. There was nobody home at Wilkins, he reported. He had his schoolbag with him and had written a note which he left on the front step, held secure beneath a stone. Then he had ridden on to Johnsons, the nearest neighbour. "The Johnsons are coming," Einar said, "but their horses are out in the pasture. He has to bring the horses in first, but they'll get here as soon as they can. They might be able to help. Their daughter Ruth is with them. She went through for a nurse."

"Oh, if they could only get here! We're helpless," said Miss Stanton.

Kirsten went outside to look for the Sandvik twins and Olise. "Somebody's coming," they told her and pointed to a car sputtering along the road toward the school. In its wake was a buggy with two people in it, the horses lashed to top speed. "That's Hallingstads," said Eric, "in their Model T."

"And Dawsons in the buggy," said Olaf. "Boy! That team can sure go!"

"Ivar must have stopped them down at the crossroad and sent them here," speculated Kirsten. "Maybe they'll know what to do."

Three adults emerged from the car and hurried into the school, followed shortly by the couple who had arrived in the buggy.

The children waited. The school door opened and the Grade Eights, carrying books and schoolbags, came out. They stopped on the front step. Kirsten and the other children went to join them. Sigrid was crying. She shared a desk with Victoria. Kirsten felt sorry for her. It must be sad to have a friend so sick. Sigrid fumbled for her hanky and dropped her books. As they were being gathered and picked up, someone noticed a loose paper covered with writing. It was handed to Sigrid. "This isn't mine." Then, examining it closer, "Victoria wrote this." She began to read.

"What does it say? Let me see," urged the others. The Grade Eights huddled closely together. Someone began reading aloud. Kirsten drifted closer hoping to hear, but couldn't make out the words. "You should give it to those inside," said Leif. "It's important." Sigrid went back inside the school taking Victoria's paper with her.

Another car drove up and Ivar jumped out followed by a man Kirsten didn't recognize. They hurried to join the group of children. "Now what's all this about?' began the stranger. "This lad tells me that someone is mighty sick."

The Grade Eights competed to tell what they knew. Now Kirsten could hear. "It's Victoria Wilkins ... she's in Grade Eight ... gopher poison ... sandwiches." More facts came out. Leif and Bjorn were privately informing Ivar. Kirsten strained to listen. Nordbys, the Wilkins' northern neighbour had taken on a new hired man, Halvor Dahl. Kirsten knew him. He was eighteen, tall and strong and had come straight from Norway to join relatives in the district. He was still learning to talk English. He and Victoria had taken a liking to each other and kept in touch by writing each other notes that they hid in a culvert Victoria passed on her way to and from school each day. Somehow, Victoria's father discovered her secret and was so angry to think that his daughter should throw herself at a stupid skywegian bohunk that he had whipped her. "With a buggywhip." Leif declared. "Maybe even on her bare ass," he surmised.

Kirsten was indignant. Halvor Dahl wasn't stupid. He was smart. And he was handsome. Nobody should blame Victoria for liking him. Everybody liked Halvor. How could Victoria's father be so mistaken? But what is a skywegian bohunk?

Another buggy arrived. It was the Johnsons with their daughter Ruth. They hurried toward the school, but the stranger intercepted them. "Tell the folks in there that I'm out here with a car and a tankful of gas. I don't think I can be of any help in there, but I'll wait here to see if I'm needed." Kirsten was a little disappointed. She had thought that maybe Ruth Johnson might have come in a nurse's uniform, but here she was wearing just an ordinary dress.

The door opened again. It was Sigrid. She was still crying. The other girls gathered around her. Some of them were crying too. Kirsten's throat was tightening and she could feel tears gathering in her eyes. She didn't want to cry. She looked for Eric and Olaf. They were throwing stones at a fence post. They didn't seem to care that Victoria was so sick.

The door opened again and Mr. Dawson and Mr. Hallingstad came out. They seemed to know the stranger who was still waiting. They spoke in voices so low that Kirsten couldn't hear what they were saying. Then Miss Stanton came out and called the children to her. "It's getting late. It's already after four o'clock. Miss Johnson has taken charge and we are doing all we can for Victoria. You should all go home now. If you're not home soon, your parents will begin to worry. So please hurry along." Then she went back inside.

Ivar helped Leif and Bjorn hitch their horses to their buggies. "Aren't you going?" asked Bjorn.

"Not yet," replied Ivar. "I think we'll wait for a bit."

Kirsten and Ivar watched the other children drive off. Now they were the only ones left. Kirsten didn't want to leave. Maybe Miss Stanton would still come home with them. They waited.

Mrs. Hallingstad and Mrs. Dawson came out. They spoke briefly to their husbands and the stranger. Mr. Hallingstad accompanied the stranger to his car and cranked it for him. The stranger drove off with the Dawsons soon following in their buggy. Mrs. Hallingstad continued talking to her husband. Ivar and Kirsten drew closer. Mr. Hallingstad seemed angry. Mrs. Hallingstad seemed to be trying to shush him. Kirsten wondered what he was mad about. Mrs. Hallingstad turned away from her husband and came toward the children. She held out her arms and drew Kirsten to her. "Victoria died a few minutes ago. There was nothing we could do to save her. Ruth Johnson helped all she could, but the poison had gone too far. Victoria sat up and said, 'I'm going to meet Jesus,' and then she died. She's in Heaven now."

Mr. Hallingstad was wiping his eyes. His voice seemed gruff. "Come along, Ivar. I'll help you with your horse. You'll want to get home before dark. I s'pose you have some chores to do."

Kirsten had forgotten the chores.

Ivar replied, "Yeah, we have to bring the cows in before supper. Me and Kirsten. They're away down in the far pasture."

"You don't want to be looking for them in the dark.

And your mama will be waiting for you. She'll think you got lost." With Ivar following, Mr. Hallingstad led the way into the barn. A moment later, they brought Thor out and proceeded to back him between the buggy shafts.

Kirsten protested. "But Miss Stanton is to come with us. To stay overnight. We mustn't go home without her."

Mrs. Hallingstad took Kirsten's hand. "Miss Stanton has had to change her plans. Because of Victoria. She is feeling so bad right now. Tell your mama that we'll take Miss Stanton home with us and then drive her over to Wilkins' a little later on. Tell your mama too that Mr. and Mrs. Dawson have already gone over to Wilkins' place to be there when they get home."

Kirsten found herself being helped into the buggy. Ivar was already there. They started off. The sun was low in the sky and the breeze felt cool. Kirsten shivered, then looked at Ivar. "Ivar! Your coat!"

"I know," said Ivar. "But how could I get it?"

Kirsten was dismayed. His new coat! And such a nice one! Would Mama scold Ivar? Could he ever wear it again? Would it be proper to wear a coat that someone had died on? Poor Ivar! She hoped Papa would buy him another.

Thor farted. Ivar swore and lashed him with the loose end of the reins. "Get going, you stupid horse! Get going or I'll show you!" A surprised Thor spurted ahead. Ivar lashed him again. Tears ran unchecked down Kirsten's cheeks. The perfect weekend would never happen. She would never think T G I F again. They drove on in silence.

But something more was bothering her. "Ivar?"

"What now?"

"Are we skywegian bohunks?"

Swan Song

Philip Westgate found immense satisfaction in being just who he was.

Philip Westgate. Everything about him was ... well, simply marvellous. Except for one thing: his immediate surroundings. Philip's nose wrinkled as he looked about the room. Even when it was new, there could have been little that was regal about Regina's Prince of Wales Hotel. And now, after nearly a century of exuberant misuse by generations of rough-shod sodbusters, the establishment's most outstanding feature was its vile reputation.

His eyes roved around the room and took in the limp curtains, a crookedly hung picture and the cigarette burns on the dresser and carpet. A steam radiator clanked and gurgled, reminding Philip of the intense cold outside. "At least it's warm in here," he thought. "With that big winter fair on, I was lucky to get even this. Imagine having to spend the most important time of my life in this wheezy, run-down old whore of a hotel. But surely, the CBC people will understand."

He caught a glimpse of himself in the mirror, and as he usually did, stopped to admire what he saw. A slim six-footer. Blonde hair, thick and curly. He ran his fingers through the curls and smiled to see them snap back into place. Eyes as blue as cornflowers, he had been told. A nose, noble without being the least bit aquiline. A lean face and a commanding jaw with a beguiling cleft in its middle. And the mouth. He caught his breath. "Mmmm! That smile and those teeth!"

He was a small-town teacher who didn't want to be one and who daily gave fervent thanks that he didn't look at all like one. His ambition was to be on display before a larger audience, an audience in the theatre; if not as a performer, then as a director, a producer or some lesser functionary. Anything would do to begin with, just as long as it got him out of that stultifying classroom and into the world of dreams — the world of music and drama. And he was very good at both. He smiled complacently. The musical that he had written and put on at Swan Lake had turned out to be such a smashing success. They entered the Provincial Drama Festival and won top honours, due mostly to his songs, especially that crazy novelty song, "Wild Oats." The cast had had such fun with it. They weren't very good singers, but the song was terrific, and now the CBC was interested in him. Their reply to his letter had stated that some Toronto brass were planning to be in Regina and would find time to interview him. He might be on his way out of Swan Lake and Saskatchewan forever. "Wild Oats" could be his swan song. He smiled as he envisioned his future greatness.

But the CBC team were very busy and on a tight schedule.

A tangle of conflicts resulted in cancellations and delays. It had finally been decided that the only opportunity for the interview would be early the following morning before the CBC people returned to Toronto.

Philip was ready. He had driven in from Swan Lake the day before — a good day's drive even in summer and nothing to be trifled with in this January cold snap. He had taken time to think about what he should wear. Dark suit, tie and cufflinks? For a morning breakfast meeting? He didn't want to look either dapper or too formal. Jeans and sweater? Maybe too casual for a job-seeker, even with the CBC. That morning he had passed by a men's wear store where he found exactly what he wanted: an Irish tweed sports coat. It looked perfect with his charcoal slacks and cashmere sweater. It had taken him the rest of the day to find the right shirt, but there it was on the dresser, propped against the mirror and gleaming in its cellophane wrapping. He hoped he would meet at least one woman on this CBC team.

If only he weren't staying in this fleabag hotel. But surely they would understand. They would know the circumstances. Maybe they're not much better off themselves. But not likely. A big corporation like the CBC would have all the drag necessary to find good hotel rooms for its executives. He knew that they were planning to take him to the airport for breakfast. Fine. An earlier plan that had had to be abandoned was for them to have dinner downtown that night. In anticipation of the dinner, Philip had bought a bottle of single malt scotch so that he would have something ready to offer if they happened to come up to his room. "Can't go wrong with a good scotch," he thought. "It will show them that I'm not a complete bumpkin."

What to do before bed? Philip looked around. Two chairs. A broken TV. Waste-paper basket. The bed, of course. A table with a telephone and an ashtray. But what an ashtray! It was a massive glass octagon. "Good heavens! Where could they ever have found something like that? I could wash my feet in that thing." Beside it was the bottle of whiskey. He wouldn't need it now. Too bad. It was expensive. There wasn't much use in keeping it for his return to Swan Lake. There was no one there to share it with. Those peasants drank nothing but rye.

Philip picked up the bottle and studied the label. What was so special about a single malt? Anything besides the price? Maybe he should try it. A generous nightcap might be a good idea. But he would need some ice.

Room service? Probably not in this dump. Philip thought he had noticed an ice machine at the end of the hall. He went to the door and peered out. Yes, there it was. The corridor was very quiet. He listened. There wasn't even the murmur of voices. He felt for his room key and then remembered that it was in his overcoat pocket in the closet. Why bother locking up? The ice was only down the hall. He kept the door ajar with the heavy ashtray and, plastic ice bucket in hand, strode toward the ice machine.

There was no ice. The machine wasn't working. There might be one on the next floor. The stairway was right there. Should he go down or up? Philip chose up.

Two minutes or so later, with ice-bucket filled, he was back on his own floor hurrying toward his room. As he neared, he heard something that made him stop. A cough. Had it come from his room? He thought so. He eased forward and listened. There was the scratch and flare of a match being lit followed by a muttered oath. It was his room, but whoever it was wasn't lying there in ambush. Maybe someone from Swan Lake. He pushed the door open and walked in.

The intruder was a woman dressed in baggy jeans and a puffy blue windbreaker. She stood with feet astride over a cardboard carton of beer, the top torn open to reveal bottles gleaming darkly inside. She was trying to light a cigarette, but couldn't manage to bring the match to her cigarette end before the flame went out. Philip knew he had to take charge, so spoke out masterfully. "You shouldn't be in here. Get out this instant!" He almost stamped his foot.

She bleered at him and swayed unsteadily. "Light me this here cig'rette."

"Certainly not! Now get out of here."

She didn't like Philip's tone of voice. She stood a little more erect and even squared her shoulders. "Light me this here cig'rette."

"No. You'll have to clear out of here. Right now." Philip confronted her directly. She was anything but pretty. Black hair was pulled back into a ponytail. Steel-rimmed spectacles sat askew on a round fat face that was nestled into the upturned collar of the windbreaker. There were scratches and traces of blood on her face. The cigarette protruding from her mouth was scorched. Taking it between index finger and thumb, she removed the cigarette from her mouth. Philip could see that a front tooth was missing.

Her voice rose. "You gonna light my cig'rette?" She fumbled with her box of matches and matches spilled out onto the floor. She returned the cigarette to her lips. She seemed to be daring him not to light it.

"All right. I'll light it for you. But then you will have to go.

You can't stay here." He knelt to pick up some matches. He lit one and held it to the end of the cigarette. The woman sucked hungrily until the cigarette was lit and then took several more deep puffs. Philip recoiled. He had never smoked. He thought the smoke would dull his teeth. "All right. That's it. Now will you please leave?"

She eyed him speculatively and grinned. Philip could see that there was more than one tooth missing. "Hey, you're cute. Let's have a party. I got beer."

"No. There will be no party. I don't want your beer. Take it and go. Right now."

She didn't seem to hear. She glanced around the room, puffing smoke in every direction, then went over and sat on the bed, continuing to draw heavily on her cigarette. "What's your name, eh?"

"George," said Philip. "Now will you get out of here?"

"I ain't goin' nowheres. It's cold outside. An' we better drink this here beer." She fumbled in the carton, pulled out a bottle and extended it toward him. "Here, open me this beer."

"No. You can't drink it here. You'll have to go somewhere else. Now go!" He thought about throwing her out. Could he do it? She looked tough. He shuddered inwardly at the thought of shouts and screams. Several Swan Lake families were in Regina for the fair. Maybe some had to stay right here in this hotel. The front desk should be able to help. He picked up the telephone. There was no dial tone. "Oh darn! What else can you expect in a place like this?"

He went over and stood before her. She looked up, grinning amiably, and patted the space beside her. "Okay now, let's have some beer, eh." She hitched herself sideways a little to make room. "We'll have a real good time. Jus' you an' me eh." Philip seized her by her upper arms and tried to pull her to her feet. She grabbed his forearms and pulled back. There was a brief tussle that Philip knew he would lose. He broke free. "Don't mess with me, big boy. Just open me this here beer. There's some for you too."

"I don't want your beer. I just want you to go. Why won't you go?"

"I got no place to go. An' it's cold out there. You gonna open this beer?" Bottle in hand, she drew her arm back as if to throw. "I'll throw it right inta that mirror."

Philip capitulated. He had noticed a bottle opener fastened to the bathroom wall. He took the bottle into the bathroom. When he returned he saw that the woman had removed her windbreaker. He set the bottle on the table, picked up the jacket and threw it into the hall. She reached out to take the opened bottle and returned to her place on the bed. Gesturing toward the beer carton, she grinned again. "Help yourself," she invited and then tipped her bottle to her mouth and drank. When she finally set the bottle down, she wiped her mouth and chin with her forearm. "My cig'rettes are in my jacket. You better get 'em."

"Nothing doing! Get them yourself."

She stood up and pulled back the sleeves of her sweat shirt. Her arms were scratched and abraded. Then she raised the waistband of the shirt almost to her neck, revealing a bare belly and breast also bearing the scars of battle. "I'll say that you raped me. The cops'll throw you in jail."

Philip retrieved the jacket and tossed it to her. "How did all that happen?"

"We had a fight. Me an' that guy. He wouldn't pay me. He couldn't do nothing an' figgered he shont hafta pay."

"What guy?"

"That guy who took me here. He wouldn't pay, so I punched him out. I took his beer too." She nodded several times for emphasis.

"I'll pay you to go. How much would it cost you to take a taxi home?" Philip took out his wallet and extracted a twenty-dollar bill. "Will this get you home?" He held it up for her to see, but pulled it back barely in time to evade her attempt to snatch it from him. He put the money away. "Now don't try any more tricks with me. My offer is still good. I'll give you twenty dollars if you leave, but you've got to get out of here first. I'll give you the money out in the hall."

"I got to pee first." She went to the bathroom and closed the door.

Philip acted swiftly. He propped the door open again with the ashtray, scooped up her jacket, the loose bottles and the carton, grabbed the bottle of scotch and ran with them out into the hall where he set the lot on the floor out of reach from his doorway. He fished the twenty from his pocket and put it with the beer, making sure it would be visible from the doorway. Then he hurried back into the room and waited for the woman. She seemed to be taking a long time. He returned the ashtray to its place on the table.

Finally she emerged from the bathroom. Philip couldn't hide his excitement. He felt that he had won. He stepped grandly to the door and seized the knob. He motioned for her to come and look. "Now here's the deal. Your jacket, the booze and taxi fare are all out there on the floor. All you have to do is go out there and pick it up." He swung the door wide open.

They both looked out. There was nothing there. Some-one had taken everything.

Ablaze with sudden anger, she turned on him. "You think you can trick me? I'll show you." And she plowed into him, striking and kicking. Unprepared for the sudden violence, Philip retreated back into the room. He tripped over something and fell to his knees. Before he could regain his feet, she brought the ashtray smashing down on his head. Again. And again.

Early the next morning, the desk clerk was responding to a police officer. "Well, you never can tell. He's been here a couple o' days. He was in and out a few times, but I never saw him with anybody. I thought he was here on bona fide business and not just to sow his wild oats. But now we'll never know."

About the Author

Conrad Romuld was born on March 16, 1926, on his parents' farm near what was then the thriving village of Dunblane in west-central Saskatchewan. The ninth of ten children born to Norwegian immigrant parents, he was young enough not to be concerned about or even especially aware of the hardships and uncertainties that beset his elders during the "dirty thirties," but was still old enough to enjoy the vibrant community life so characteristic of rural Saskatchewan at that time.

He obtained his Grade Twelve standing largely through independent home study and went on to study English Literature at the University of Saskatchewan and at Leeds University in England.

After University, Romuld enjoyed a long and varied career in public education. He and his wife Rita have three daughters and three granddaughters. They currently live in Saskatoon.